First Printing, 2021.
ISBN 13: 978-1-84481-169-4
ISBN 10: 1-84481-169-7

D1824300

Published by New Line Books, London

Warning and Disclaimer
Although every precaution has been taken to verify the accuracy of the information contained herein, the author and publisher assume no responsibility for any errors or omissions. No liability is assumed for damage or injury that may result from the use of information contained within.

Every book I write owes a lot those around me. The ones who put up with my insane questions and outlandish suggestions. And that special person who has to suffer through my moods as I strive to make the writing in my mind to become the words you read. You all know who you are. Thank you is never enough.

Intentional

How To Live, Love, Work and Play Meaningfully

David Amerland

New Line Books

London

New Line Books

Permissions

Acknowledgements

There is no such thing as an original idea or a novel thought. Some things may be articulated first by someone and their articulated synthesis may be such as to make them feel fresh and original but their seeds have come from somewhere external. Everything that comes from inside our head has been put there by the external world.

This time round a great many brilliant people contributed in some way to my thinking. Some did so consciously in open, involved discussions over Zoom and Google Meet over a period of months. Others, shaped my thinking with their comments, reactions, suggestions and ideas. Others still, live their life in an intentional way and, to me, they became a source of inspiration.

So, in no particular order, my deepest gratitude to Ron Serina, Bruce Marko, Gina Fiedel, Bruce McTague and Zara Altair.

My deepest thanks also to Eva Goldstein whose editing sharpened up my prose when I faltered and whose questions helped make this book better than I expected.

If you come across any of them in social media give them a shout out. They fully deserve it.

About the Author

David Amerland is a Chemical Engineer by training who specialized in quantum mechanical perturbations in laminar flow processes, before stumbling into the world of search engine optimization (SEO), social media marketing and branding via mathematics. He is the author of over a dozen books on business, marketing and search including *The Tribe That Discovered Trust* and the best-selling *Google Semantic Search*. He writes for Inc., Forbes, and HP UK and blogs extensively on his own website, DavidAmerland.com. When he is not writing or surfing the Web he spends time giving speeches internationally on how search, social media and branding are changing. His last book, *The Sniper Mind* became, for him, a deep dive in the world of neuroscience, critical decision making and brain analytics and their application in real-world business.

Praise for "The Sniper Mind"

"The first word that comes to mind after finishing this book? Wow. Just wow. Insightful, engaging, extremely well researched, and very well written. And now, for the meatier review.

"When I first stumbled across this book I was skeptical. While I saw that the author was well reviewed for other books, those books were about SEO and marketing, not the military, personal development, leadership, or any other topics running rampant through these chapters. But after having the book in my cart for weeks, going back and forth on whether to pull the trigger, I did, and I'm so glad I made that decision."
— *Sara, Amazon Review*

"I recommend reading this book. The sniper stories act as a kind of fuel that keeps you moving through it, so it ends up being a quick read. Over the course of reading this book, you start to put together a much better understanding of how it is that the human mind can be trained over time to accomplish amazing feats and perform on a whole new level."
— *Gideon Rosenblatt, The Vital Edge*

"As a former Navy SEAL officer and FBI SWAT operator I've had the distinct pleasure of working with snipers over the span of 20 years. David's assessment of how the sniper mind works is as good as it gets. More importantly, he gives hope to those looking to tap into the psyche of these amazing individuals. This is an absolute must read for anyone looking to become better in any aspect of life."
— *Errol Doebler, former Navy SEAL, former FBI Special Agent, and founder of Leader 193*

"*The Sniper Mind* book is power. Key success factors are delivered to you in a great way that enables readers to blow up their professional and personal barriers! This is a terrific approach to cognition and perfectly in line with what I've learned over 30 years, moving from elite combatant to entrepreneur, where mastering anticipation is a silent weapon, and empathy and perspicacity are ammunitions."
— *Michel Reibel, Former Sniper, Strasbourg, Alsace, France*

"I strongly recommend the book to all who understand how difficult is to be active in business today and who need support, guidance and examples."

- Mirek Sopek, President, Makolab

"Being a former sniper, I was immediately attracted by the book's title. I was under the impression that this book was an in depth look at what makes snipers tick. It is, however, once I began reading *The Sniper Mind* by David Amerland.I realized it was about much more than snipers. Although the author examines how and why snipers are so successful at their craft, he then uses their techniques and tactics to illustrate how anyone can be successful in life by using the same techniques snipers use."

- John Willis, Officer.com

"Having read it, I've been finding myself more ensconced than before in learning (and choosing to learn) how to break down, analyze and apply the granular components that lead me to deeper understanding of how I operate day to day. And then how I can make better use of my in-built natural resources and grow useful new skills through a distinct brand of honesty that comes with this kind of scrutiny. I have found that my perspective is transforming. It's almost like being re-introduced to myself."

- Gina Fiedle, Fat Eyes Web Development

"I used *The Sniper Mind* to change the way I run my business. A lot of the things we do in business life involve making decisions that are critical when we are under pressure. Our emotions guide us before our brain kicks in. Learning to understand and manage this process better, improves the choices we can make and the outcomes we can get. It's not a magic fix, but it is a much-needed boost in creating the type of awareness that business leaders and entrepreneurs need in order to enjoy greater success."

- Brandon Matthews, CEO, Office Solutions

"Confidence, in turn, contributes significantly to our sense of control over our life. A sense of control is what allows us to critically examine and adjust our beliefs, hold firm to our core values, develop the right kind of attitude and display grit when we need it."

Table Of Contents

How To Use This Book

Considering how a book, by definition, presents a body of writing that is to be thought about as it is being read and after it is read; having a "How To Use This" section seems oxymoronic. It isn't. Being intentional in life means being in control. This is not the same as having control of everything and everyone or being controlling.

Psychology sees a sense of control as having freedom to choose and a sense of agency. Neuroscience regards control as having "neuroanatomical correlates of the sense of control: [with] Gray and white matter volumes associated with an internal locus of control".

Whether you personally feel that the brain and mind are separate or that the duality of mind and body exists is immaterial here. The fact remains that when it comes to taking responsibility over our choices and control over our direction in life you will need to experiment to find what works best for you. The experimenting, I hope, will change you and the change you experience will guide you.

This book then gives you all the parts but not the whole. It gives you the science and my own thoughts about it based on reading countless studies. It gives you the direction but there is no prescription and certainly there is no formula. Instead what you get are eleven chapters, each representing a trait, attribute or modality that affects how the whole functions. How you function.

You can dive into any chapter in any order or pick each one sequentially. It really depends upon your own needs and inclination. Whichever way you choose to tackle it, what you must absolutely do is look at the *Points To Remember* section at the end of each chapter and ponder on the three questions asked, afterwards.

Those three questions are your scalpel. They will help you peel back your own unique anatomy and discover how to make yourself tick better.

Finally there's the *Top Tip*. This is usually the last point in each chapter. It is always practical and you can put it to use straightaway.

My Story

My story barely matters. Yet as the author of this book, now it does because you, the reader, require at least some context in order to decide whether what I have to say is going to be of direct value to you. One side of my life and career is very much like anyone else's. Another side, obviously, isn't. I will focus, mostly, on the latter.

From the moment we're born we are all biologically designed to do the same thing: survive. To do that our brain collects information from our senses and then uses that information to establish a sense of space, a sense of self and a sense of context. But the senses, on their own, are relatively limiting. They contain us within the boundaries of our sense of touch, taste, smell, hearing and vision. In time, these become the first sense we receive of a world around us and a sense of self within us that shows us that we inhabit that world.

We intuitively know the world is much bigger than that however. We know that it can also change faster than we can experience it; it can present unexpected threats as well as rewards and it is run by rules that are based on the physical reality that we experience. To augment our abilities we then couple sensory acquisition to information retrieval (and I apologize in advance about search engine vocabulary here), which is what we call memory and knowledge.

Memories allow us to store experiences and ideas and bring them up as required to help us better understand the context of particular moments in time. Knowledge is a qualifier. It helps us determine not just the potential of harm or reward contained within each moment (which, inadvertently impacts on our motivation), but also the underlying ground rules that help us establish expectation and understand nuance.

Knowledge is the ingredient inside our head that when it's mixed with memories and senses; creates in the context of the moment the option of understanding what could happen next.

Our ability to predict the next moment in our life with some degree of certainty allows us to get out of bed in the morning, to make plans for our next birthday, to dream of a better life, to plan to create a better world. The skills we use here, even at their most refined, are relatively linear. We analyze, learn and make predictions based upon the particular combination of sensory input, memory and knowledge we have achieved. The means through which we do so is governed by the direct experience we have of doing so.

So who we are, who we might become, where we fit in, how and what options lie open to us in the future; are governed directly by our upbringing, circumstances and environment which, in turn, govern our identity creation and identity curation efforts. It is important to note, even this early on, that these two things are not always in alignment and from their misalignment frequently stems cognitive dissonance that consumes a lot of our mental effort and physical energy because both consciously and subconsciously we strive to reconcile the two.

This brings things back to me and my story. Unlike the majority of people I experienced, from very early on, cultural shifts in my identity because my family travelled. My mum and dad not only changed geographical locations which meant that I had to get used to new people, different surroundings and new friends, but also countries. By the time I was 20 I'd lived in three countries and two continents.

Like every other person who's experienced this kind of mobility in their formative years I found myself without the opportunity to put down cultural roots. I had no extended family and I fully expected to leave my friends and favorite places behind without warning. Psychologists generally agree that frequent relocations are bad for children's wellbeing. In a study that involved 7,108 American adults who were followed for 10 years the researchers found that "children who move frequently are more likely to perform poorly in school and have more behavioral problems."

Dr. Shigehiro Oishi, of the University of Virginia, who led this study, went further in his analysis looking at attributes in adults such as life satisfaction, psychological well-being and quality relationships. What he found was that for introvert-type personalities frequent relocations during early childhood resulted in a stunted adult emotional and psychological life. As the study progressed it also appeared to negatively affect their lifespan most probably because relocating is stressful and stress tends to affect a person's health and reduce their ability to fend off disease and the ravages of ageing.

Extroverts, on the other hand, appear to have a much easier time of it, mostly because they have fewer difficulties in making new friends and finding a social circle to belong to.

If you ask me I am an introvert. Yet I have none of the psychology-defined attributes of an introvert. I am insanely curious about my surroundings, I find it easy to make friends and I find it easy to integrate myself in different social constructs. Without going into too much detail in the still on-going debate about whether the definition of introverts and extroverts is correct, I personally ascribe the discrepancy between my self-reporting and what a trained psychologist would perceive in the way I relate to the world.

Like an introvert my frequent relocations when young have robbed me of a deep sense of belonging and the expectation that what I do and where I live are permanent. That doesn't mean I don't have a deep need to belong and the need to feel that my surroundings are well enough understood as to be safe for me. Bereft of a tribe made up of people I expected to see most of my life and without the background of growing up with them or having shared the same local culture I became adept at picking up commonalities and using them to integrate myself in the community I find myself in.

Psychologists will most probably recognize the adaptive response and explain my extrovert behavior as a direct result of it. By making friends easily, quickly finding a way to be useful and deliver value and being open and accessible I substituted 'local' for 'global', joining whichever group of people I happened to find myself with. At the same time I found it easy to pick up the similarities in the cultural patterns I encountered which I could then use from my experience to determine how to best behave.

Psychologists make it sound a little too contrived. I understand that my brain developed this approach because it was deprived of the traditional option of developing a familiar tribe comprised of family and childhood friends and colleagues acquired through life in one place or, at the very least, a particular geographic area. I also feel that I truly love people for who they are. I am amazed at the openness, brilliance and warmth we're capable of and I truly love the fact that culturally we all want the same things even if local conditions have led us to develop different ways of trying to get them.

None of this blinds me to the fact that we can also be dangerous to each other and the planet, narrowminded, biased and occasionally so short-sighted than we can be convinced to act against our own best interest. That, however, is also part of the magic of us. I see it as a common vulnerability we all share that marks us as members of the human race. The fear we feel in the face of uncertainty, our constant search for easy answers, are things we have all felt at one time or another and most feel still.

My experiences and the initial accident of my being, haven't made me necessarily smarter or wiser. They have made me however a little different. And I have always mined this difference to be of as much service to my world as possible.

This book is the result of my personal journey. It is the outcome of a lifetime's effort to be part of a grander whole because circumstances usually made it impossible to be part of an immediate, local one. In writing this book I have, as always, sought to provide as simple an answer as possible to a complex question. The question is: How do I live on purpose?

It's not an easy question to answer. Most of us fail to live like we really want to, in the way we want to because it really is a difficult thing to do. It requires effort and energy when we are really hardwired to avoid both.

By providing a simple answer to this complex question I have hopefully helped lessen the cognitive and energy load of living a purposeful life. In that case you will find it easier to do so. This will benefit me as well as you because, in my mind, you and I share the same tribe and are part of the same global picture.

So, thank you.

David

1.　Life

Here is the first truth in a book of truths: you can't be everything to everyone. At some point you need to make a choice of what truly matters to you and why. Fair warning: it's an approach that will lose you a lot of 'friends'.

There is little point in trying to define what 'life' is. Philosophers and, surprisingly, even some biologists, have never agreed on it. Biology however tells us that life is: "defined as any system capable of performing functions such as eating, metabolizing, excreting, breathing, moving, growing, reproducing, and responding to external stimuli." The moment you think about this definition you know that there is little point in trying to adapt it to concepts such as "living a good life" or "a life well-lived", yet it is by those that most of us intuitively try to measure and understand what it is we mean when we mention "life".

As it happens I will give you a much better definition but before I do I will start with an obvious truth: we all struggle with the exact same thing that is, knowing how to behave.

In trying to live a life, good or bad, we all seek to find, discover or accept a set of rules that basically tell us how to behave in any given situation. When we accept social mores, religion, the law, tradition, culture, a code of conduct, a belief or an ideal what we basically engage in is a direct attempt to find our personal rule book that tells us exactly what to do when we need it.

I am a sucker for mindless action flicks that spike my adrenaline levels and shower me with eye-candy special effects. If you've never seen *Wanted*, starring Angelina Jolie, James McAvoy and Morgan Freeman, then I strongly recommend it, not least because in one of his over-the-top cinematic speeches delivered with that all-too-familiar authoritative deep, tonal voice Freeman's character declares:

> *"Insanity is wasting your life as a nothing when you have the blood of a killer flowing in your veins. Insanity is being shat on, beat down, coasting through life in a miserable existence when you have*

a caged lion locked inside and a key to release it."

He goes on to give the requited spiel about a fraternity of super-assassins that take it upon themselves to guide history by killing selected people "for the greater good" and he finishes it with the memorable line: "This is what has been missing from your life Wesley: Purpose." I did say it's over-the-top. At the same time the speech has a point. A life lived without a purpose is a life mostly wasted. And purpose is frequently defined by knowing what we should do and being actively engaged in doing it.

Whether we realize it or not, we all feel the need for this kind of guidance that gives us a deep sense of purpose. Because we are born physically helpless we have evolved to latch onto and work hard to understand our immediate environment and the people around us. This makes us, as we grow older, intensely pro-social. At the same time it provides us with a ready-made set of expectations, rules and guidelines to guide our behavior that arise from the collective behavior of those around us.

That behavior is the culture we experience and the traditions we abide by. The problem with this is that rather than defining for ourselves what is important to us we accept that which is given to us. That which is given to us is rarely what we want, but it can very easily become what we settle for.

Settling is an evolutionary-programmed trait. Let me explain: Life is hard. It really is. Even if we happen to have the extraordinary luck to be born into a very rich family whose legacy gives us everything we need to live comfortably for the rest of our life, maintaining that fortune and navigating through life is going to be fraught with risks, traps and constant upheavals.

We need other people. Other people need us. That is a truth. But the reasons for this mutual need are usually contradictory or, at the very least, sufficiently at odds with each other to make trust an issue and turn cooperation into a risk-assessment exercise.

All of this takes inner resources. It takes attention, thinking, planning, mental and psychological effort, perhaps some introspection. It frequently is emotionally painful and psychologically costly. We are programmed to avoid it because it adds to the intrinsic difficulty that is life.

If you want the definition of life here it is: It is a game plan that emerges from the collective activities for survival of everyone around you. That is, everyone. It is difficult because it is unpredictable. It is unpredictable because no one knows the rules. In an emergent game plan things change spontaneously according to the same principle that guides us to settle for what we are given: conservation of energy. When 'witches' threaten our communal beliefs, the stability of our governing institutions and the perceived natural order of the Cosmos it is required of us to hunt them down and publicly burn them.

The act, however, barbaric, painful and seemingly inhuman restores the perceived natural order of things, reinforces the power of our institutions to safeguard our way of life and impresses upon us the value and desirability of accepting what we are given. Life goes on much easier then.

When the public burning of witches however marks our way of life as brutal, our religious leaders as misguided, fanatical zealots whose actions endanger us all and our institutions as unbending, power-hungry instruments of control, we become more enlightened. More accepting. Our society becomes tolerant. Our horizons broader. Life goes on much easier then.

"Easier" is what we have been programmed to seek because it increases the chances of our survival. What made sense in pre-historic times when the outside world could easily kill us has, in our days, evolved into a complex dance of what we believe and what we reject, what we accept and what we actively seek. We have created a world that pretty much guarantees our survival. Yet, for most of us that is no longer enough.

We lack the deeper sense of purpose that makes us feel truly alive. We have the key to releasing the "lion" inside each of us but choose not to use it. This makes our life a complex weave of small advances and retreats. Victories and losses that are designed to keep us in place until we no longer care and it no longer matters.

I say "designed" when I describe the constant churn of victories and losses that are life, but that is a mislabel. Life is a system. Like any system it seeks stability in order to function. Stability demands conformity. Almost like a biological organism, the system that we call "life" rewards innovation and change (i.e. mutations) sufficiently to progress but makes it hard enough for them to become established so that it is never severely disrupted.

It is no accident that in our lifetime we shall each experience only one great innovation or upheaval. More than that and it may truly be the end of the line for the experiment called "Human life on Earth".

This need to live by choosing "the path of least resistance" because it allows us to use the least amount of energy to coast through life leads to some pretty convoluted mental acrobatics. We are, for instance, perfectly at ease with a Dr Jekyll and Mr Hyde transformation where we present a different face (and maybe, even values) to those we work with and a completely different set of behaviors to those at home or our friends at the pub.

We can use 'morality' to ostracize and dehumanize fellow human beings who are different from us, because their existence creates perturbations in the social system we directly experience that require greater energy in order to deal with and may, even, challenge our own sense of right and wrong with our own life choices.

The ease with which we can turn on anyone not of our own religion, social caste, skin colour, ethnicity, neighbourhood or area is testament to this. History supplies a long list of such instances that range from the destruction of Carthage in pre-history to the genocides that took place in Rwanda and Bosnia in the closing years of the last century. In each case the ingredients are the same incendiary mix of social stress, political polarization and a dehumanization of the 'other' that is different, strange, outside our own group and therefore the enemy who deserves to be eradicated.

The irony that this is the same game only with different players escapes its participants who had they been capable of such awareness would have behaved differently anyway. The irony is rich here because in order for this game of life called "division" and "ostracism" to work its players must be capable of exhibiting the same behavior when confronted with the same set of circumstances. The oppressed turn oppressors just as easily as the victims can turn into aggressors. Given similar circumstances and capabilities we are usually pretty good at coming up with justification of our behavior and if you need a living, breathing example of such role reversal look at the atrocities, injustice and demonization of the 'other' carried out by none others than the Israelis upon the Palestinians.

A case of role-reversal, where those who history has frequently ascribed the role of victims turn into aggressors and perpetrate on their neighbors the same type of persecution they have, historically, experienced themselves.

Now that we've established, on these broad lines, that life is a game whose rules are the same everywhere and we have seen, again broadly, how similar circumstances allows us to behave in similar ways and even make the exact same behavioral mistakes we, ourselves, have condemned it's fair to ask "what now?" Is this it? Will this chapter be enough to raise questions without providing much of an answer¬? Is everything always grey and in doubt? Is the rest of the book more of the same which would make it no more than a superfluous addition to this chapter required to provide what publishers call "spine value"?

Well, not quite. What follows are the elements, the modalities, if you like, required to make this game of life work. What follows is the prescription you need to live your life the way you want to. This chapter, however, is far from over.

Because all this is serious I can afford to be flippant, though as you will see even my flippancy has a very serious intent. So, I will add here that the one 'rule' we all need to keep in mind is that favourite of William S. Burroughs' from his *Naked Lunch* "Nothing is true; everything is permitted". Burrough, of course, borrowed this from Vladimir Bartol, who used it in his novel *Alamut*. Bartol, himself borrowed it, and slightly changed it in the process, from the teachings of Hassan-i Sabbah who was the founder of the Order of the Assassins, historically known as the Nizari Assassins. The tale, writings and doctrine of the Order was incorporated in the storyline of the popular video game *Assassin's Creed* which is where I first came across it and filed it away for future reference which brings us to here and now. You reading what I've written.

What do we, what can we learn from this? That life is circuitous but the circuit has polygonal junctures with cultural jumps and bends that require an open mind and a thirst for cultural learning in order for the metaphorical dots to connect? Or, that nothing is truly original, that everything is borrowed from somewhere else and made to fit the moment and its time?

Both, I'd argue. If you are truly living and if you truly feel alive you are aware of both context and history. Moment and time. *Alamut* was written as an implied rebuke to Mussolini's fascism. *Naked Lunch* is a chronicle of the messiness of life and its often unplanned trajectory where the brain makes sense of basically senseless moments of existence. This book is about learning to behave in ways that help you get more out of your life. Each of these is the product of the needs of its time and though we may repurpose the same material in some form, the recipe, each time is fresh and poignant. Palatable exactly because the circumstances have called it into existence.

Consider the simple proposition that everything that stands alone is a piece of information, a datum. An event, an occasion, a concert, an idea even. Put a lot of these together and you get data. Data requires action; we all need to somehow respond to it or do something with it or do something to it. Actions give rise to culture. Culture, in turn, is affected by context. Context changes the value we ascribe to data by making us re-examine the facts and what they mean to us, right now.

Fig. 1-1. Our decision-making process uses a calculus that takes into account the sensory input gathered by our body, our understanding or acceptable norms, traditions and collective behavior and the relative uniqueness of each situation we find our self in.

Rebel With A Cause (Or Without)

If you're reading this and you're young then you already know the feeling inside you that wants you to become a rebel. It doesn't matter what it is that you want to rebel against or fight for. You just want to fight. If you've been young (and we can all claim that) then you are already familiar with that feeling and the nagging remnants it leaves behind that make you, on occasion, behave in ways that your critics call "out of character".

The idea that someone other than yourself has a better grasp on what your character is and can then judge your behavior as being in tune with it or not is ludicrous at best, delusional at worst. Yet this is exactly what people will do, not realizing that what they are actually judging is not your behavior according to your character but your behavior according to what they want your character to be. And the reason they want you to be in the character they ascribe to you is because it makes life easier for them.

By accepting what they give you and behaving accordingly you reinforce their own value judgements and life choices. You validate their beliefs. You live according to their expectations. You, in short, then are not "you" who thinks and acts but the "you" they want whose thoughts and actions fit a pre-moulded idea that generates the least amount of trouble for the greater group you belong to. Live like that and you will find that your life will evolve into a series of steps, actions and calculations designed to keep you contained within the "least troublesome" subset of society, generally labelled as "respectable".

"Respectable" comes with assigned, pre-determined and carefully bounded social status. That social status is automatically given to you alongside the perception of a pre-assigned social value. Accept both of these and you only need to put up with whatever personal unease you feel about your life choices, until you die. At which point the people and circumstance that ascribed all this to you, and you who chose to unquestioningly accept it, no longer matter.

This way each generation tries to forge its own way but only truly ends up re-asserting the status quo. We each become our parents because we become parents in turn. We end up shoring up the creaking structures of our societies because we set up our own edifice of personal value upon them which then makes us have a vested interest in their stability.

Just like Flat Earthers cannot prove their proposition, no matter how hard they try, using the existing science that has already proved the Earth is round, so we cannot hope to truly change our life if we only use the values, roles and attributes that are ascribed to us by those around them.

Unlike Flat Earthers however we stand a chance to design, create and use our own sense of right and wrong and our own set of values.

Why? For the same reason we do anything even when, in our journey from early youth to mature adulthood, we are destined to fail. For control. We want to control our world because a sense that we are the one in control goes a long way towards assuaging the deep sense of unease we grow up with.

Decision Making, Data and Culture
(how actions generate data that leads to culture and creates context)

"The first step — especially for young people
with energy and drive and talent, but not money
— the first step to controlling your world is to
control your culture."
Chuck Palahniuk

Decision making		
Data	Culture	Context

Data gives rise to culture, culture creates context but context changes (the value of) data

Data	Culture	Context
	Style & Tastes	Ideas
New Gen		Values
	Music & Art	Beliefs

Fig 2-2. Ideas, values and beliefs create the context through which we filter everything.

If we control our environment (by establishing, accepting, reinforcing and championing) its values. If we control our life (by living inside the grooves already carved out for us by the 'system') we then control the unexpected. We ensure our survival. We reduce all potential hazards that may threaten us.

Or so we believe.

Some people may, consciously, believe this. Others may just tacitly accept it. The fact that acceptance, tacit or otherwise provides us with a sense of belonging goes a long way towards quietening the shrill alarm bells that ring inside us, the constant sense that the world is unstable, dangerous, potentially cruel, inherently unjust, and downright dangerous.

By wrapping ourselves in the delusion of stability and security, acceptance and belonging we manufacture a reality that shields us from most of the difficult things we should have to do long enough for us to get old and die before it becomes imperative that we do them.

We are all rebels for a while because neurobiologically we all sense the work that is to be done, the values that we must really get behind. The wrongs that we should fight to right. Then, we grow up. The system we fought to change engulfs us in its embrace, smothers us with its insistence and we become what we once resisted.

Depressed? You shouldn't be. That is the natural order of things given our relatively short lifespans, even shorter memories and the tiny window of time and opportunity we have; to achieve happiness, enjoy good health and create wealth. All these elements only add to the sense of stability and security that leads us to accept what we are given.

Human motivation leads to actions that take us from a place of relative discomfort and anxiety to a place of less discomfort and less anxiety. Neurobiologically this decreases the energy cost of staying alive. This makes us happier. Happiness is weird. It doesn't always follow logic, it's not linear in cause and effect. It doesn't appear to always follow culture or traditions and sometimes it even goes against our, immediate, self-interest.

Yet we seek it because of the way it makes us feel. And the way we feel is mostly everything to us. Here's a truth: the past holds us captive. Even when we succeed in giving up slights, grudges, feuds and pride, we cannot easily give up knowledge, memories and experience. Neurobiologists tells us that the sum of our knowledge, memories and experience create our perception. Our perception shapes our expectations. Those expectations, pre-load behavioral patterns in the brain that guide our behavior.

What emerges from this is the realization that when those patterns do not get pre-loaded, our expectations subside and our perception changes. We then end up with behavior that is guided by the direct circumstances we encounter in the context they happen in. In a different setting we might call that living in the moment or a Zen approach to life.

I cover happiness in the last chapter of this book. Exactly because of its complexity and all the other chapters that must precede it in order for it to make sense. I am not going to jump the gun here so I won't say anything beyond what is necessary for me to say in order to explain why we do some of the things we do and why we react the way we do.

To do that I must explain what life is and how entropy figures into this. To avoid the heavy mental lifting that this approach requires I will stick to simple explanations and provide, as I usually do with my books, a full bibliography for the research referenced in each chapter.

Why Are You Alive?

No one knows why you are alive. In case you're inclined to take this personally find momentary assurance in the fact that no one knows why anyone of us is alive. You can take this value statement at a metaphysical, philosophical level or the more prosaic level of biology and chemistry and it will still be true. Sure, there are a lot of theories that range from the strict self-reliance and self-governance of cynicism (the philosophical movement, not the attitude), to the logical positivism of Wittgenstein and the embodied cognition of cognitive neuropsychology but none has risen beyond the level of theory. There is a lot to recommend each one and that's even before we begin to consider the teachings of the world's many major and minor religions.

There is no way to examine 'truth' here. They are all true. Or they are all false. It doesn't matter. The moment you find something that works for you, it works. That's all that's required. So, if we're not going to even try to tackle the meaning of life why do we bother asking the question of why we are alive? That's because life itself, the state of being that allows me to sit in front of a digital device and type in words which at some point in my future you will use some other digital or otherwise device to read, is still being debated over. We are not sure how we transition from inanimate matter, a bunch of minerals and chemicals mixed in with some water, to a living, functioning being. But transition we do. The transition allows us to examine, physically, what life is as opposed to non-life which means we can also determine what it is that marks us as being alive.

Technically speaking everything in the world is a system. Life is no exception. All systems are governed by two things: A. Their energy state. B. Their level of stability. There is a push-pull dynamic between these two. Technically speaking, again, the perfect balance between these two is one where the energy state we experience, guided by the fundamental requirements of physics is so low as to be perfectly stable.

Unfortunately, that is technically called rigor mortis and it's the point at which life stops and we revert to the relatively inert form of the chemical building blocks we are made of.

Life, as we experience it, requires that we are in a constant state of energy harvesting. If we take that to its logical extreme we may end up having short but glorious lives. We shall constantly be looking to consume enough food and nutrients in order to do more and more, build more and more muscle and be as energetic as possible. Unfortunately, that also makes it possible for our body to burn out and our cells to go wrong and become ill enough to kill us.

In order for us to remain as healthy as possible the body struggles to remain in a position of stability. The balancing point of this, however, is always moving. The energy expenditure we undergo in our teens and twenties is not the same we experience in our sixties and seventies. And yet the body has to find a way to balance everything so that we remain in an energy position that is stable. It does this despite it having to undergo repairs, build muscle, maintain processes that keep us alive, deal with unexpected emergencies and keep fatigue at bay each day long enough to ensure its physical survival.

To explain precisely how all this is done we normally need to have some understanding of evolutionary biology, classical biology, quantum chemistry, classical chemistry and physics. For our purposes however we need only concern ourselves with physics and, in particular, with thermodynamics and within that branch only with its second law that basically describes how heat (i.e. energy) flows in a system. The second law also introduces the concept of entropy which is a physical property of thermodynamic systems which makes it a physical property of every system in the universe.

Entropy is a measure of disorder. So a high entropy environment has a high amount of disorder in it. Like a derelict house that has finally collapsed (or a human body that has stopped being alive), the maximum amount of entropy in a system presents us with a stable energy configuration that can remain stable for a pretty long time without any input from any outside source.

Since entropy describes how energy flows in and out of a system (and even explains why it does so) it is a fundamental law of the universe. We are kept alive because we are governed by three distinct characteristics which also determine what it means to be alive. They are:

- Energy harvesting behavior
- Self-repair (and reproduction)
- Computation of the future

Think about how you go through your day to sate your hunger for food: You most probably begin with breakfast before you set off for work. Your body processes the food you've eaten to help you accomplish the physical and mental tasks that constitute your day. At the back of your mind you've already planned or are in the process of planning what you will do in order to get lunch.

This is the simplest sort of generalized human behavior we can use. It contains all three of the characteristics required to define life.

There are countless examples of machines, programs and constructs that can perform passingly well one or maybe two of these functions, but no system can perform all three and not be alive. The reason we are looking at what it is that makes you alive however is because whether you like it or not these three characteristics are at work regardless of whether you are aware of them or not.

We all need to eat, have a need for sleep and potential mates. And we all then look for the means to remove anxiety from obtaining our next meal (and maybe mate) and our next opportunity for sleep. Conscious awareness of what drives us, how it works, what effect it has on our thinking and behavior and the fundamental universality of these driving forces is the first step towards actively guiding our choices so that our decisions are intentional.

Meaning To Life

I fully understand that "meaning to life" is not the same as me giving you the meaning of life. That is something that I can't do because I can't, in all honesty say I have it. At least not in a generalized enough sense that would apply equally to everyone who reads this book, which is what an all-encompassing, comprehensive, detailed explanation of the meaning of life would have to do in order to stand up to scrutiny.

What I do have however is my personal definition of meaning to my life. That's synthesized by my own experiences, upbringing, beliefs, perspective, identity, values, goals, aims, dreams, hopes and direction in life.

While it is next to impossible for anyone to arrive, at least for now, to a definition for the meaning of life that would be universally accepted the same cannot be said for giving meaning to life. The scope here is much narrower though no less personal. The distinction makes all the difference. The meaning of life has to weigh everything you are, define your purpose from birth, guide your every action in relation to a universally accepted cause and be, virtually every respect, your moral compass and guiding star.

Meaning to life comes from what you do, how you do it, how much thought, planning and effort you put into it and why you do it. It stems from your values and goals, aims and principles. It defines who you are and what kind of world you visualize around you. Meaning to life arises out of the effort you put into creating and maintaining relationships with your friends, it springs from the times you do the right thing when no one is looking. It is composed of the occasions when you did something that was the right thing to do or benefited a wider group of people, even though for you it was difficult.

In short, meaning to life is what you create out of behavior, thoughts and actions that have real meaning to you and those around you. It is what develops from living intentionally as opposed to just being dragged along by the tide of people around you and their lives.

Acting so that there is always "meaning to life" is hard to do but not impossible. Because none of us is immune to being carried along by the people around us, remaining steadfast in our attitude of acting with intent and living with meaning demands that we choose to surround ourselves with people who are at least as intentional, focused and determined to make their lives count, as we are.

To briefly recap: Adding meaning to life requires that we are intentional. Being intentional adds meaning to life. I am aware of the solipsism here and the perfection of the argument I've just constructed. I draw special attention to it so that you're not fooled by it. Your life is your own. Only you can make it count. Things that count always have a cost. Determine, for yourself, what you are willing to pay for the values you believe in and act accordingly.

Life is complex. We are complicated. There will be times when this value statement will be reversed. What will never change however is the sense of satisfaction that comes from being the sole architect of how you choose to live.

If you accept what I've just said you may find it enlightening, thrilling, illuminating and empowering. It may touch you deeply enough to change your perspective, transform your thinking and change your life (and I will be truly thrilled and humbled, if that's the case). If you don't accept what I said, for reasons of your own, you will become combative and attempt to dismiss it as only my opinion; a prescriptive, narrow perspective drawn from someone who's already admitted in this chapter that he's not qualified to philosophize about the meaning of life.

First, either response is fine with me. It is your life. Only you can choose how to live it. Second, as with every book I write; my opinion, thoughts and ideas are supported, in part at least, by research and the opinion, thoughts and ideas of others who're better qualified than me on the subjects I draw material from.

I would urge you to explore the bibliography I supply.

What Can You Do?

Having just said that you can, if you really want to, choose to live your life intentionally and with meaning, now I have to, at the very least give you a couple of practical ideas on how to go about doing so.

There's nothing metaphysical about meaning in life. But there is a necessary synthesis that takes place from the physical: physical health. The mental: cognitive health and sharpness. And the psychological: identity, goals, achievements, aims and a sense of purpose.

Studies that have looked at groups of people in different age groups and longitudinal studies of the same people have found that the search for meaning in life is associated with an awareness of the lack of meaning in life and it is then linked directly to a decrease in personal happiness.

Unhappy people suffer socially, physically and mentally.

The same studies have found that there is a correlation in the feeling of helplessness and a lack of aim we feel in our youth when we still try to workout who we are and what we want to do and our final stage in life when we have lost friends and family due to age and disease and we no longer have a job to define our sense of purpose and make us feel like we still contribute to society.

Identity and purpose are key to both. We all experience some cognitive dissonance as we try to align our inner beliefs and principles with what we need to do in the external world in order to survive. To minimize that feeling we obviously need to reduce the gap between what we feel, what we think and what we do (and why).

Try this easy form of self-analysis:

- Write down one instance when you acted completely according to your beliefs. Detail what it was, when, where. How did it make you feel?
- Now write down what you think would be needed for you to always act that way. Detail the requirements you see into four groups labelled: material, emotional, psychological and social.
- Check to see which of these requirements are accessible to you but you don't use them or haven't thought of activating them and which are completely out of your reach.
- For the ones that are out of your reach (if any) which can be replaced or substituted by something else?

The problem with being intentional, no matter what level you decide to exercise it at, is that it requires you to be aware of what you do, the impact it has and the responsibility you then carry. This is hard for several reasons. Some of these we will explore in greater detail in the chapters ahead but a quick recap here will help us understand some things better.

Introspection is painful. We are good at lying to ourselves. Being honest, even when it is just inside our head activates painful realizations and memories. It takes an enormous amount of energy to deal with all this. We usually tend to avoid it.

Discipline is hard. It requires constant reinforcement and real reasons to keep it going. We really can't do it alone, we need some kind of external help in the form of friends who think and act like us or a mentor to help us maintain our focus.

I will close with two truths. One, so intuitive that I barely need to articulate it: No one really knows how to live and everyone feels guilty about something.

Two, Nothing lasts forever. Not even we.

The second one is what should drive us to be better each day for as long as we can. The second truth is what we should remember as we strive to be intentional in our thoughts and intentional in our actions so we can be intentional in our life.

Points to Remember

- Nothing is new in our life or the world about us. Yet everything is unique. Context supplies the novelty factor that changes everything. Tradition, history and culture are interpreted differently in each context.

- Every revolution, in time, becomes what it has overthrown. Every child, becomes its parent but *only* if the child becomes a parent in turn.
- Something is considered to be alive only if it meets the three requirements of harvesting energy, self repair and computation of the future.

Question Time

- Are you happy with your life as it is right now? If not, which is the one thing you can realistically change that will give you a greater sense of control?
- How do you plan your life? Maybe do not and cannot plan every tiny detail, but how do you plan the strategic direction and aim of your life so you can guide your self in the different situations that you encounter?
- How do you define value in your life? What is it that you constantly need to, or try to build so that you can feel your life is worth it?

Top Tip

- Create a safe space and a me-time for your self. It can be anything, from a retreat in the mountains with a yoga group to some time spent in the gym with your headphones on. The point is to take yourself away from the constant demands made by those who surround you and the life you have and do something that is just for you and makes you feel good about yourself and, hopefully, also gives you a little respite from life and the opportunity for some self-reflection.

2. Identity

If you truly know who you are, if everyone around you really knew who they are, then all of us would know what we want. A deep sense of our own identity produces a sense of values. A sense of values dictates a sense of direction. A sense of direction helps us prioritize the things that are important to us. Prioritizing what is important to us helps us decide how to best allocate our mental, emotional and physical resources.

The allocation of our mental, emotional and physical resources helps us understand how to behave. Nature is governed by physics and physics explores the fundamental laws of nature. We are all part of the natural world and are governed by the same laws of physics as everything else around us. This makes us an integral part of the universe. It also makes us weak, which means we are fallible.

"Know Thyself" was the inscription, in ancient Greek, welcoming dignitaries, kings, emperors and statesmen to the forecourt of the Temple of Apollo at Delphi. In the ancient Greek world it was the place so many people of power visited seeking validation for their mission and guidance in their actions. Hoping that the words of the oracle of the god, known as Pythia, would take away the need for them to search for who they truly were, the forecourt's admonition notwithstanding, and become who they thought fate and the will of the gods warranted.

It is ironic. By abdicating their responsibility to act on their own and accepting the consequences of their actions they allowed their actions to decide who they were. Actions require energy. Energy is what our mental, emotional and physical resources run on. Its allocation always reveals what we value, who we are, what we prize and what values we hold.

Here is a fact: we have evolved to deceive others. It is an evolutionary survival trait that allowed those who could successfully hide their motivation and camouflage their intentions, gain a competitive advantage over their rivals that allowed them to survive. Even if, pre-history is a lot less bloody and cruel than we may think it is, being able to successfully deceive is the means through which the human brain understands what is required of it in order to guide the body to fool animals that used to be our prey.

Gifted with speed, size, a sharp sense of hearing and smell, I imagine, that our prey was designed to avoid danger and either outran or overcome a species that had neither speed nor strength to help it in its hunts. But that species did have another advantage. One that nature doles out sparsely and which we have refined with time: cunning. Hiding behind it, deceit.

The brain doesn't develop redundant circuits. To do so is too complex and energy intensive, two qualities that make long-term survival problematic. Cunning and deceit practised and honed in hunts is a transferable skill that can be applied in tribal group settings and social gatherings alike. Today we are all versed at telling 'white lies' and projecting an image that may not quite corelate to reality. A cursory skim across a Facebook or Instagram feed is rife with both of these examples of human deceitful behavior.

From there it is just another short leap to telling an outright lie and actively, consciously deceiving someone for personal gain. I don't want to make this sound like a 'slippery slope' sermon or even imply that because we engage in the first set of deceitful behavior we naturally will engage in the second. Far from it. The subset of people who earn the right to wear the label of 'liar' as a characteristic of their general behavior is small indeed.

Nevertheless we all have the capacity to lie and the ability to deceive. And the most successful practice of both of these occurs when the target is our own self. We lie to ourselves all the time through the ever-fluid editing of the narrative of our conscious life. Fans of the Christopher Nolan film, *Memento* remember how the film's protagonist, played by Guy Pearce, reconstructs his memories through notes, clues and tattoos he's left for himself so that he can understand his motivation and complete his 'mission'.

The film leaves open the possibility that Pearce's character, Earl, may not be what he appears, that his quest may be a fake cover story to protect himself from the personal consequences of his own actions and that his entire, constructed narrative may be a fabrication.

At the end of the film the audience, already involved through the mutual 'discovery' of clues the director intended for them to find, is now left wondering whether everything was false. They doubt themselves, their interpretation of what they'd seen and the film's initial narrative arc.

Our own life story is no different. Left entirely unchallenged by reality we are all capable of fabricating details, altering the chronological order of things, magnifying or downplaying our role in events. All, to best suit the constructed narrative of self.

Research in patients who have suffered life-altering, traumatic events reveals that our sense of self is, indeed, a construct. Indisputable as that may be it is hard to ascertain exactly who or what creates that construct and how it is done (or why). If this were a detective novel and the construct was a witness' alibi the lead detective in the case would have a hard time accepting it as real. Lacking an understanding of the mechanism of its construction, a means of independently verifying the facts and a way to understand why it was constructed in the first instance he (or she) would reject the account as "unreliable".

Yet, here we are. The unreliable (but from a personal point of view, undeniable) construct of self we experience is what we each have to work with. Hence, this book and its chapters. The core thesis here is that if everything we label "consciousness" is made up of constructs that rely on perception, memories and awareness then by better understanding the recipe of that we create a multi-prismatic lens that allows us to be more guided, more directional and more intentional in who we are and where we end up in our life than if we allowed the tide of life to carry us, like so much flotsam, to wherever it carries us and deposit us to wherever it wants to deposit us.

I know the imagery I've just used conjures chance and helplessness. I am not advocating doing nothing in fear of doing the wrong thing. Doing nothing in your life is the same, in terms of decision making, as choosing to leap into a roaring river. You may not control the elements or what happens next or where you will end up, but you will struggle nevertheless while in it and you will fight for survival and you will end up feeling you've done 'something' by the end of it.

Rivers and life have trajectories and rules that guide their dynamic evolution.

The difference between the choice of leaping in or not, of doing something meaningful or letting the tide of things carry you along, lies in the value you decide to place on the things you want to achieve and your willingness to accept the price for their achievement.

Margaret Robinson, a widely acclaimed British molecular cell biologist who is a professor and researcher in the Cambridge Institute for Medical Research, at the University of Cambridge had this to say when she was asked about what drove her:

"There is nothing more exhilarating than to find out something for the first time – something that may have existed for over a billion years, but was never known before."

Why should an awareness of knowledge like she just describes makes us all feel and understand her excitement? Her sense of purpose in life? Maybe because the ability to discover such knowledge and then 'own it' gives us a sense of control. For Robinson a sense of purpose and control over the world at large, for us a sense of control in how the world works.

If we can better understand something we can control it. If we can control it we can master it. If we master it, it no longer has the ability to surprise us or frighten us. Do any of us consciously start each day with the clear intent to understand the mechanics of what is happening around us and the reasons behind it and then bend everything to our favor? I'd say no. Yet, our brain has evolved through countless permutations and over hundreds of thousands of years to do one simple thing: help us survive.

That's the brain's Prime Directive. To do this, the brain only has one true function (let's call it its Prime Function): predict the next moment. If somehow, at birth, we were all given magical crystal balls that could foretell, precisely, the next moment for us a lot of our issues with identity, many of our neuroses and psychoses and insecurities would be solved.

We'd know exactly how to behave because we'd know in advance what would happen next. Imagine taking this superpower into the tricky field of dating. No more rejection (and what it engenders). No more uncertainty over whether we'd be able to hook up with a person or not, which means we'd have to also stop trying to impress them by projecting an unrealistic image of ourselves. No more worrying if we are good enough or striving to garner sufficient attention through our achievements so we can be deemed "attractive" and desirable as potential mates.

All we'd have to do is check to see what would happen if we approached a particular person and if the magic crystal ball we held told us it would be a negative outcome then we'd move on confident that we would soon find someone else. Even our sense of disappointment, in that context, evaporates.

We would stop trying to get jobs we never stood a chance to get. We'd stop attempting to do things we cannot do. Living in a world of certainty much of our fear and anxiety would disappear. Trust in other people would come down to asking our magic crystal ball specific questions in specific contexts. We'd stop worrying about life being uncertain and maybe, even, our search for the meaning of life would become moot. I mean if all we had to do is move safely, to the next best possible moment for us why agonize over greater context? Why worry about who we are? Or, what we want? Or what it all means?

You can see, I hope, how much we are impacted by the uncertainty of the universe and by life's imprecise trajectory. The question is why? Why does uncertainty, which is a norm in the world, impact us so deeply that we forget who we are or neglect to ascertain who we are or fail to even grasp that we have to discover who we are?

The reply to that question is given by the brain itself or rather its Prime Function. As the brain tries to predict the next moment it basically becomes a prediction machine. To function as such, it needs to have a grasp of motivation (ours as well that of others), trust, perception, the concept of the past and the idea of the future alongside an awareness of the present.

These are complex, fluid elements that require massive amounts of computing power to calculate. Compared to the size of our body, in the mammal world, we have the largest brain. It consumes almost a quarter of our daily energy needs. To give you an idea of the size of brain we have consider that a fully-grown sperm whale that weighs 57,000kg (125,663 lbs) has a brain that's just 9kg (19.8lbs) in weight. The average weight for a human being, globally, is 62kg (136lbs). If we were as large as a sperm whale and our brain maintained its proportion, it would weigh 1,419kg (3128lbs). Almost a ton and a half.

Our brain is so large compared to our body size precisely because we use it as a prediction machine to navigate the immediate future. The fact that we are still here is testament of its exceptional ability to do exactly this.

The brain's singular purpose however expresses itself through, and utilizes many other abilities: meaning-making, organization, projection, analysis, intuition, decision-making, narrative-creation, empathy, deception, model-building and focus. I haven't tried to exhaust the list here or even organize it into categories that separate skills from attributes.

Neuroscientists, increasingly, view the brain as part of an extended network of information input. The body's sensorium supplies some of that information but that is nowhere near enough for the brain to function and us to become aware of who we are. Sleeping, waking, seeking comfort and avoiding discomfort, feeding, mating, rinsing and repeating is something that even the amoeba does. So, for us it's not enough.

We need other people, relationships, friends, groups, entertainment, art, culture, science, quests, adventure and struggle to feel alive. The brain, acting in its predictive machine capacity seeks to absorb as much information as it possibly can. In that respect it engages with the world. And by engaging with the world it uses its many information channels to absorb everything it needs in order to think and help us become who we are.

In short, the definition of who we are happens through the looking glass of our viewpoint of the world around us. One of my favorite poets is W. H. Auden whose devastatingly accurate poem *Law Like Love* explores the definition of law (and our understanding of it) through different professions, people and levels of education and attendant social status. The point of the poem, at least in the way that I am using it here, is to show that we see what we expect guided by what we know.

The less we know the less we understand. We may see exactly the same things as someone with more knowledge and awareness than us but we interpret what we see through the lens of our own narrow experience and understanding. To understand more we need not just to see more, we already see enough, but to broaden our interpretation by broadening our understanding of the world and, by association, our self in it.

They say "travel broadens the mind" for a reason. Travel exposes us to cultures and people outside our direct, personal experience and that makes us recalibrate how we see the world.

We Are What We Know

Notice a couple of provisos in my proposition here. First that knowledge is accompanied by awareness. Awareness, in its simplest explanation, is the perception that something else exists relative to us. This relativity allows us to ascribe specific values to each of the things we know. Those specific values, in turn, become an ever-changing matrix we use to determine who we are, how important we are and what the world is.

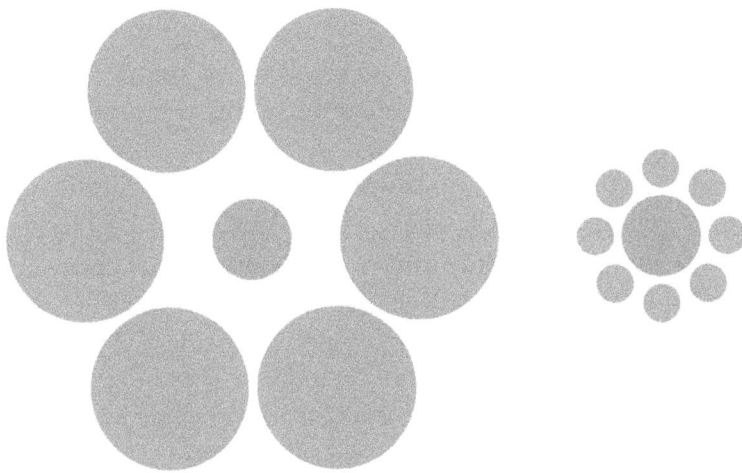

Fig. 2.1 – Which central circle of the two shown here do you believe to be the largest?

I cannot, here, resist the opportunity to express this whole sentiment visually by introducing an optical illusion favored by neuroscientists who study visual cognition, known as the Ebbinghaus illusion or, sometimes, as the Titchener circles.

If you're human and you look at the two circles of the Ebbinghaus illusion you will clearly pick the one on the right as the larger of the two. Here's the rub however: they are both identical in size. When optical illusions trick our mind to see something that isn't there (in this case size) they also reveal how the brain processes information.

The Ebbinghaus illusion shows that when it comes to size the brain, lacking precise, mechanical measuring equipment, calculates the size of everything by running it through a comparison filter with its surroundings. Elephants are pretty big mammals but next to a sperm whale they appear tiny. A sperm whale is huge but place it alongside the *USS Nimitz* and it too, appears tiny. Place, however, a human in front of this lineup and you begin to realize just how big elephants are.

This relational and therefore semantic weighing of size in the brain adds extra depth to the casual saying "everything is relative". As far as the brain is concerned relative values deliver the context of the moment. The context of the moment creates perception. Perception shapes reality.

Before I digress too much I will circle back to my earlier qualification that you will see the circle on the right the larger of the two if you are human. As it turns out those who study canine cognition have proved that this is an optical illusion that dogs don't fall for. They can actually see that the two circles are equal which means that at least within the context of comparative size dog's brains are wired to see size for what it is.

Knowledge held inside a brain means nothing if it cannot be shared in the brain's extensive, detailed network and utilized in various ways to help it make sense of the world. This is where awareness comes in.

Don't fall into the trap to assume that awareness is the same as consciousness and that since you are a conscious being (as, you assume, I am) then we are both aware.

Does your smartphone have feelings? Does your dog? Most people will answer "No" to the first question and "Yes" to the second confident that they are self-evidently right. Without going into too deep an analysis, most people assume that feelings are the result of the complexity of our inner world and our intelligence. Dogs, they will argue, are not as intelligent as people but they are undoubtedly intelligent beings. Just like people, they feel things and we know that because they exhibit behavior that we can interpret as joy, anger and sadness.

Yet, from a purely data-processing capacity point of view your smartphone is smarter than your dog. Sure, you may bristle at the suggestion and point out how your dog is aware of its surroundings whereas your smartphone is not. That, however, is wrong too. Your smartphone, through its GPS signal, is in constant communication with the cell towers around you and, if you're at home, there are a number of apps and other services, including Google search, that track movement, speed, location and habits to pinpoint exactly where you are and, sometimes, what you are doing.

Your smartphone then is more aware, way more precisely of its surroundings and location than your dog. Moreover, in an incredible display of crossover communication, it can understand some of the context of our needs when we use an app to access a service (like Google search, Uber or Tinder) much better than most other humans, never mind dogs.

The point is that consciousness is really hard to determine and does not rely on awareness. Thankfully, identity is much easier to understand.

There is a second proviso to knowing who you truly are. And that is that identity, even after it has been ascertained, is also fluid because it is relative to our external world and that external world is always changing.

Would the uber-criminals and villains of the fictional *Suicide Squad* become heroes if the world around them didn't become a much more risk-fraught and dangerous place to live? I'm not going to answer this for you. If you haven't seen the movie, why not? What exactly are you doing with your life?

That, actually is the question we are each trying to answer when we try to understand who we truly are.

Knowledge, tethered to awareness allows us to understand how we got to the point we got to and why. That awareness, applied to the knowledge that the external world is fluid and uncertain and we adjust, somewhat, for it also allows us to anchor our identity in values that can guide our decision-making and actions, better.

The Yin and Yang Of Self

We are each the product of two worlds. Both exist in us but not in the same amount. In some of us they are perfectly held in balance. In others one or the other takes over for a while and then the tables are turned and others still one or the other world completely overwhelms us.

The two worlds? The external and the internal.

The external world is what gives us our ascribed identity. We are, say: "White, Anglo-Saxon Protestant". Or, "husband", "son", "daughter", "housewife". There are a myriad labels we can apply and each of these represents something that comes with its own set of rules and expectations. "The prodigal son" in a family operates under different restrictions and capabilities than "the darling daughter".

We come into this world with brains largely blank. Not knowing who we are, what we can do, what we are capable of or what we should aspire to. There is an entire, richly layered set of norms, values, morals, laws, boundaries and controls imposed by family friends, society, the country and propriety that will guide us through the majority of our steps, if we only let them.

The internal world gives us our avowed identity. That's the 'dream' of who we want to be and what we want to do. Ironically that too is informed by a significant amount of data that reaches our brain through the outside world but it also fits in with what we feel inside our head and how we see ourselves.

What we feel is always a little bit of a mystery for everyone but us. How we see ourselves is also highly personal. What we feel is partly the result of the way the brain interprets the data from all of our senses and partly the result of how successful we become at bridging the gap between our sense of who we are and what we want to be with what the external world demands of us.

How we see ourselves is the product of how we balance our dreams, capabilities and potential against our understanding of the world and our place in it. A prisoner serving life in the dark side of the moon might want to give up dreams of surfing waves in Hawaii. In practical terms this would serve his situation better. Acceptance would make him happier. But that is not how it works.

Dreams and hopes keep us alive. They take the raw material of the uncertainty of the world around us and they fashion a cognitive mechanism that allows us to contemplate possibilities that will keep us from giving up being alive and dying or falling into dark despair.

Note that in this journey of identity there is "better" but no "best". Knowing who you truly are, knowing thyself in other words, is better than its opposite. But becoming who you want to be versus becoming who everyone else wants you to be is not "best". That's because "better" is a relative value which we can ascertain by comparing how we feel about our self and our achievements against our inner hopes and dreams. "Best" is some subjective pinnacle that represents the end of the road. There is nowhere to go from there.

It goes without saying, but I will articulate it here regardless, if you truly know who you are, then you know what you stand for. Knowing what you stand for makes your life meaningful because your actions become intentional even if the world is fluid, uncertain and ambiguous.

But how? How does anyone do that, exactly?

The Manual Of Who You Are

Ideally, there'd be a hefty manual we'd each be given at birth. That way by the time we reach chapter 18 in our teens we'd know what to do in order to turn into fully-functioning, well-adjusted individuals who seek to contribute to society as we further strive to develop and perfect our self.

Unfortunately, such manual exists only on our expiry date and we have written it ourselves. The problem with this approach? We have 20-20 vision only in retrospect. In our journey we will make mistakes, fail often, get discouraged and disheartened even when we shouldn't. And learn the lessons we should with great difficulty.

Is there some way to avoid all this? To avoid the self-inflicted blindness at times when we need clear vision? To avoid the muddle-headedness and woolly thinking at times when we truly need mental clarity? To avoid taking blind alleys in our life thinking they're paths that lead to our goal?

Lacking said manual or a magic crystal ball (that would have been a brilliant alternative and perhaps way lighter to lug around) there is still a mechanism we can employ that will deliver largely the same results. At least some of the time.

What? You ask.

The Three Constituents of Identity

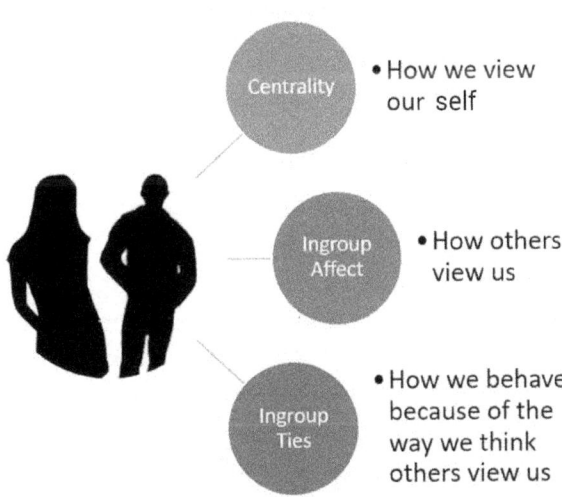

Fig 2-2. Our sense of identity emerges out of our sense of self and how the self we perceive is creted through its ties with external factors which lay claim on it.

I say: "why"?

Before we dive further into this, and we shall, I need to clarify a misconception. Being intentional in how you live is not the same as planning every moment of your life. It is not the same with being serious all the time and never letting your hair down. It is not the same with never being spontaneous or weighing every single instant of life against some carefully conceived master plan. Fun, spontaneity, indecision and a live-in-the-moment approach can still happen.

Life is fluid, often complicated and most time complex. Being intentional means you own your actions in moments when those actions count most. An accumulation of such moments leads to an intentional life. Those moments cannot accumulate if you're not consistent in your values and clear in your direction, wants, needs and purpose.

Now that this is out of the way and we both know that being intentional does not mean you have to sacrifice having fun in life, let's go and see why asking "why" is such a powerful tool in helping you understand who you are.

Peel Back The Onion

Identity is multi-layered. Not unlike the many layers that make up an onion. Despite its many layers it is made up of three elements, each of which contributes to the layers we use to create a sense of who we are. These elements are internal, external and the result of the synthesis of these two. Neuropsychologists and developmental psychologists label them "Centrality", "Ingroup Affect" and "Ingroup Ties".

U.S. Navy SEALs and Special Forces operatives everywhere instinctively understand the dynamic here. They understand that to become who they are they had to be "broken down" to their basic core. The essence of themselves that made them resilient, resourceful and willing to focus and achieve their tasks under the most adversarial of circumstances.

In Navy SEAL training this happens during the aptly named "Hell Week" which sees, on average about three out of every four trainees give up and drop out. The British SAS have an even worse drop out rate, averaging nine out of every ten candidates who initially passed the physical requirements of their course.

I am not suggesting here that you give up your job, drop out of your life and go and join the army in order to understand who you are. What

I am pointing out however is the powerful competitive advantage you gain when you truly know who you are.

Special Forces operatives are a special bunch of people. Despite the seemingly ordinary nature of their external character, those who make the grade have a fierce intensity that springs from clarity in their sense of identity. Once they understand the purpose of their mission they can become focused, clear-headed, driven and determined. They are virtually unstoppable.

Do you want to be a little like them in your everyday life?

"Why" is the surgical blade you wield to peel back the layers of your emotions and understand their source. Psychologists call this instinctive elaboration. It is what happens in the brain when it is confronted by a question and has to provide an answer to it. It activates neural processing centers that pull information from knowledge, memories and perception.

Do you feel afraid of something that stops you from making a decision and taking action?

Ask yourself "why". Start with why you are afraid. And then ask why is the answer you give yourself the answer you give yourself; what is it exactly that makes you give that answer. And then ask why is whatever causing the root of all this fear the root of the fear you feel.

You get the drift.

It's a little like saying "I'm afraid of clowns" and you then ask "why" and you have to tell yourself that you don't like the cognitive dissonance your brain gets between their seemingly happy face and what you understand to be the opposite of a person's life who is forced to earn a living by pretending to be happy all the time. And then you have to ask "why" should that be the reason and you have to say that it's because it reflects some kind of ingrained social inequality that you don't like and when you again ask "why" you have to admit that you don't like it because you're afraid that it reflects part of your life and how you are caught up in a system that makes you behave in ways that you don't like and if you ask "why" you will have to confront the truth behind what you want and what you do and the choices you made that got you there.

It is an emotionally painful process.

It can go on for as long as you are willing to be honest and willing to take the emotional pain that arises from it.

Is this beating yourself up? Well, from an emotional, experienced pain point of view it can certainly feel that way. But it is different in that you're not punishing yourself for anything. You're just peeling back the layers of who you are and that is always a painful process. You then begin to understand some of the things that are truly important to you.

Understand what's important to you and you begin to understand who you are. This comes with the added realization of quite what you are prepared to do.

The realization does help you focus your efforts better. It also helps you understand where you should not be wasting time and resources.

I'd love to say here that the moment you understand who you are everything becomes easier, but that's not true. Some things, possibly, improve; like your perception and judgement. Others do not. And maybe some things will feel worse, like the way looking at the broader picture of the world makes you feel. Accept, however, that overall this is an improvement in your cognitive capabilities and, by association, your emotional ones too.

Even worse, to some extent, you will be a slightly different person in different contexts. This is not to say that you're not being open or authentic. But your improved awareness of your identity and your better understanding of your limits also enables you to decide just how much you invest in each situation you encounter.

To hark back to my somewhat trite example, consider how understanding the root of your fear of clowns may have led you to understand how you feel about yourself and why you may now want to spend less time, for instance, partying every weekend with your friends and more time spending time further developing a hobby you truly like.

As a result you may seem less carefree to your old friends. Being intentional leads to actions. Actions always have consequences.

Points to Remember
- The brain evolved as a control system that helps its bearer negotiate a highly complex, rapidly changing and often not so friendly environment.
- The brain has one Prime Directive: to survive.
- The brain has one Prime Function: to predict the next moment.
- We all want the exact same thing in life: a sense of control.

Question Time

- Can you describe who you are in a sentence?
- Is your description of yourself consistent across all your ages (child, teen, adulthood).
- How has your description of yourself evolved over time? Why do you think this evolution has happened?

Top Tip

- Find your mantra. The one thing you can always tell yourself to raise your spirit and stiffen your resolve when things are tough.

3. Goals

I'd like nothing more than to tell you here "you're defined by your goals". Taken to its logical conclusion this is a statement that amounts to the equivalent of a "Get Out Of Jail Free" card. Not only would it be easy to change the perception of who you are by tacking in a pre-millennial Miss World-worthy goal or two (world peace and being kind to animals) but you would also be totally free of any hint of responsibility for who you are as you'd reel-off all the goals that society, your peers, your culture and your immediate family have pressed upon you.

So, now that I've crashed that subterfuge, you're hopefully asking yourself what is it exactly that should count as a goal? Obviously, anything which you set as a target somewhere in your future, that you aim to hit, is a goal. As such a goal is a desirable end result you arrive at after taking a series of actions. These actions are consecutive in nature but, depending on the nature of the goal, can have a short or long timeline.

You define your goals. They don't define you. But the goals you set always define who you will become. This is true whether you succeed in them or not, reach them or not.

In some way goals are an integral part of motivation. Motivation is the chapter that follows this one so I will try here to separate those elements that can be separated so you better understand what role goals play in your intentionality.

In a general sense we use goals to do two very distinct things: A. Give ourself a sense of overall direction in our life. B. Create hope. We need both a sense of direction and a sense of hope to continue to function in a meaningful way. So, pretty much, we all have goals. And we all re-evaluate them and re-affirm them or change them.

The countless number of people who will start a new diet "on Monday" and the millions and millions of people who publicly affirm their resolutions for a coming year do so because of this dynamic. Both "Monday" and the start of a new year are arbitrary and somewhat subjective chronological markers we use out of convention to mark a starting point of our intended productivity.

To us, as humans who need to feel that we can do something better because something else has happened that has given us a fresh opportunity, both chronological markers represent magic gateways through which the constraints of the past that held us back no longer apply.

We tell ourselves that come Monday our decision to start a new diet (or a new exercise regime) will no longer be affected by the doubts and perceived difficulties we experienced in the past. We will make "a fresh start" and the obstacles we have already encountered will magically disappear. Our unwillingness to establish a better relationship with the food we eat, for instance, or our addiction to sugar or fatty foods or an abundance of food, will magically evaporate. Our distaste for sweat, fatigue and physical discomfort, all of which are associated with exercise, will no longer matter.

Of course, we are bound to be disappointed. Despite our best intentions the diet will be cheated on, broken and eventually abandoned. The exercise regime will be circumscribed, followed irregularly and eventually circumvented altogether.

Why?

Not because we cognitively don't understand the health benefits of a well-balanced diet and regular exercise. We fail to stick to what we say because of the way we feel. More particularly the strength of the feelings we experience from a future self who is thinner and fitter are not as strong as the feelings of hunger, pain and fatigue we experience in the present as we diet and exercise.

We are designed to respond to the strongest feeling we experience. My fear of being eaten by a tiger, for example, far outweighs any distaste I may have towards sweat, the pain in my lungs as I am out of breath and the burning in my legs as I force them to move me at the fastest speed possible. As a result when coming face to face with a tiger, I will give my utmost to get away from it and get to safety. All other considerations will simply not be factored in.

Similarly, in less extreme situations than my admittedly extreme example we react to the strongest feeling we can identify in ourselves. The strongest feelings, by far, are the ones that arise from the moments we are in. Pain, fear, anxiety, discomfort are emotions that produce a strong physical and psychological response in us. We have been designed, by evolution, to respond to them. So our natural inclination and even our instinctive response is to move to take action to relieve the intensity of these emotions even if this action sabotages the goals we have set that will benefit us in the longer run.

What we feel is linked to how you feel. If we separate our mind from our senses we create internal dissonance we have to fight against all the time. This means when we most need mental resources we will find ourself short.

Yet, to be present not just in our own mind, but our own body is no easy thing to do.

Self-sabotage happens for many reasons, not least because we fail to weigh what we feel right now against what we will feel in the future. The calculus in our head that measures present feelings against possible future ones is predisposed to magnify current issues and play down future ones.

The classic (and more than a little wrong) metaphor we employ to think of the different layers, centers and functions of the brain is to separate it into three distinct, virtually independent layers, comprised of the R-Complex (or so called reptilian brain), the paleomammalian complex (more commonly known as the limbic system) and the neomammalian complex that we usually refer to as the neocortex.

This creates the impression that there is a primal part of us that takes over at times and a more refined, civilized part that is in control at other times. But the brain, just like the body, functions as a fully integrated, holistic organism.

Virtually all the higher executive functions we employ when we make complex decisions, set goals, decide our path in life and map the world and our place in it require the neocortex. This means cognition; education and knowledge. When we experience powerful emotions however, irrespective of whether they are joy or sadness, the neurochemicals that flood our system and activate the centers of the brain that create those emotions also cause a partial shutdown of the higher executive functions of the brain.

Consider the classic cliché of the absent-minded young lover whose brain is so taken over by the strength of his love that even mundane tasks become challenging. Think now what happens in a situation that has caused panic: a natural disaster or an accident. Data studies of participant responses in situations where a terrorist attack has taken place show reaction or inaction are more likely to take place as a response than considered, logical action. Almost 90% of those present will either panic or freeze. Only one in ten will keep their cool and act to maximize their survival.

While being in love and being in danger are not equal situations by any means they do demonstrate that left to our own devices the ancient responses of our brain do not always work to our benefit. Often in today's complex world, they will lead us to do things that are likely to work against our own self-interest. Even more disconcerting when challenged and in the face of overwhelming and frequently irrefutable logic and evidence, those who react in such fashion will double-down on their response, shut down and refuse to listen and respond logically.

One of my favorite books of all time is Frank Herbert's visionary, science fiction masterpiece *Dune*. In one of the opening chapter very early on in the book one of the characters tests the protagonist with a poisoned needle pressed to his neck and a test of endurance of pain. The test is simple enough: endure the pain and survive the needle. Its aim however is telling:

"Let us say I suggest you may be human. Your awareness may be powerful enough to control your instincts."

Our ability to exhibit higher executive functions in critical situations is, indeed, a test on how we manage thoughts and responses that arise out of our immediate senses and operate in such a way as to achieve a desirable outcome at a future moment.

If you've read the book the test applied to the protagonist seems to make no sense. Surely pain of the magnitude he experiences is to be avoided. After all that is what we have evolved to do as humans. The thing is that the struggle that takes place in the brain in is not so much a case of pain vs non-pain as a struggle between two reward systems. One is activated by short-term goals and immediate gratification and the other by long-term goals and deferred (or delayed) gratification.

In order to make a choice for the one or the other type of gratification the brain forces the two reward systems to compete with each other and the victor of that competition decide how we act.

There is a reason for this. Our neural circuitry is complex because in each moment different parts of the brain either cooperate or compete with each other. If I give you a creamy donut and it's Monday and you have made this deal with yourself where you can eat any sweet you want but only on the weekend, you now have to make the mental calculation where you weigh the cost and sensual pleasure of eating the donut now or throw it away because it is Monday.

Which you end up in this calculus depends on factors such as your sense of who you are, how you feel about yourself, your overall image of how disciplined you are, your specific reasons on why you don't eat sweets during the week and a large number of variables like how you're feeling being back at work after the weekend, the kind of day you are having, the time of day I offered you the doughnut, the weather and your perceived workload for the week ahead.

The point is, and we are getting back to goals, that emotion plays a massive part in your decision. Emotion is generated, in part, by the brain's processing of environmental stimuli. It is the primary driver of action and neuroscientists and psychologists see us as emotional machines that think instead of thinking machines that feel.

If you eat the doughnut I so cunningly gave you, you will exhibit a classic case of self-sabotage. That small act of eating the doughnut will open the floodgate of permission because it trains your brain's reward center to lean towards instant gratification rather than delay it. It may erode your belief in your own discipline. It could elicit even stronger feelings of guilt and self-recrimination because you broke your own rule about when you eat sweets. And this may bring about even worse responses from you.

People who set goals and never meet them or cannot stick to resolutions fail because the goals they set are so distant or unrealistic that the odds are already stacked against them. If, as another extreme example, I set myself the goal to get a bodybuilder body and you give me the creamy doughnut I know straightaway what will happen.

I will eat the doughnut.

Attaining the large muscles and lean physique of a bodybuilder requires so many hours of training each week that unless I am committed to putting them in I will never succeed in my stated goal. Deep down I know it, even if externally I tell myself I will do it. When the reward centers of my brain decide I should eat the doughnut you gave me; it is a classic case of the short term rewards center clocking a win because the long term rewards one is already working with an unrealistic case scenario, that may just never happen.

It is this setting of unrealistic goal-setting that trips us up. We promise ourselves we will start dieting "on Monday" already deferring when we will start not so we can start a diet on a specific day of the week but so we can give ourselves permission to indulge now.

We say we will stop smoking, drink less, exercise more, work harder, read more books, be kinder, in the "New Year" because the distance between then and the moment we set these goals allows us to pretend that we will do those things. In the meantime, the now is the now and we have not yet started.

When the "then" of our promise to our self becomes the "now" we inhabit we start our journey burdened by the knowledge that we will be unable to continue because we have done nothing to prepare for it or we put off the action we intended to take and find some creative excuse why we did that. Life, kids, work, study, the weather, hook up, break up, whatever. Life is sufficiently complex for us to never lack good excuses.

The Path You Choose

Now that we know the "what" and the "why" of goal setting and we are aware why some goals happen and why others don't. It's not just a question of perceived difficulty. It is also a question of feasibility, having the ability to set goals that are within our grasp.

Video gamers will recognize the three basic characteristics of an attainable goal that will keep us plugging away at it until we succeed.

- A perceived journey that enables us to either exhibit or develop mastery of what is required of us as we undertake it.
- A path where we can display our commitment to the goal. And path that is just right to make us capable of sticking at it until we succeed. Commitment is multi-faceted. It manifests itself when we feel something is within our grasp, no matter how far we have to reach. Something that will deliver a tangible benefit of sorts that will take us further along our journey and deliver us to a better psychological, emotional and maybe, even, material place.
- The final component is competence. There is a fine distinction between competence and mastery. Both have to do with capability. Competence however is incremental. We become competent at performing specific tasks, for example like finding toe holds in sheer rock faces, developing grip strength and setting pitons, which when taken in their totality exhibit a mastery of a specific activity like rock climbing. If the goal we set ourselves to

achieve doesn't help us gain competence it will be a waste of time and effort.

It is no accident that the same three characteristics, with some cosmetic differences in application, crop up when we discuss resilience and how to develop it. Because life is complex, messy, and resistant to organization and planning metaphors serve us better than prescriptions on how to live it.

Goals are waystations. We get to them with some effort and at each point of achieving them we are given the opportunity to enjoy a brief breather before moving onto the next one. But as waystations, they only add up to some kind of sense if getting to each of them takes us in the direction we want to go towards. Otherwise, we are lost.

Being intentional in our goal setting is not about being ultra-regimented, hyper-disciplined, detailed in our planning and rigid in our execution of it. Maybe some moments, in a specific context, can be like that. But life, as a whole is chaotic.

This is not just a supposition.

Consider that the world is a system. Within it everything else is also a system and that includes you and me. And each system is governed by its own logic that makes sense only when it ensures the long-term survival of the system. There is an inherent dynamic to each system and that dynamic changes significantly when one system interests with another.

Think how, for instance, the grass on your front yard seeks to maximize its sustenance, spread and grow, taking over more and more area in front of your house and capturing more and more nutrients from the soil and sunlight from the sun. The system that is the operating system of the grass regularly intersects with the system that is your house which is bound, usually, by some local, legal constraints that stipulate the appearance of your lawn and the look of your house. Consider also how that dynamic is further compounded by the infusion of the aesthetic principles of you, personally which will play a determinant role in the look of your lawn and your activity in its upkeep.

The system that is your operating system tells you that having a well-manicured, green lawn makes you feel better about yourself and your choice of house. It makes you feel better about your perceived social status amongst your neighbours and those who pass by and see your house. That, in itself, is yet another system governed by commonly agreed values and culture-driven awareness of what's important to us as individuals who have chosen to live in a greater society.

The analysis is far from complete. Yet, you already see that each of these complex systems has its own logic and internal workings. The point where they intersect, combine, occasionally merge, cooperate and occasionally compete with each other, creates the wider machinery of what we perceive to be the world.

The popular notion of this collective, gargantuan structure is that "the world is a cold, cruel place". This is wrong. The world is an amazingly complex, beautiful structure that emerges out of the synthesis of what is nature and what we put in place through our ingenuity and technology. But it is largely uncaring of us because it barely notices us.

To matter; to feel 'warmth' and 'care' we need to be noticed. We need to feel we are heard and that we count. The world automatically will not do that. Its complexity appears chaotic because much of its machinery, both natural and man-made, is misaligned and competing more than cooperating with other systems around it.

To picture it, imagine a six-lane freeway with three lanes going either way. If you try to cross it without looking you will most likely get ran over and be killed. Yet you don't want to die. Each motorist in each car does not want to kill you. But the system that is you, in this case, is trying to do something at complete odds with the system that is the motorway that's designed to funnel cars in a particular direction, at speed. The desire of each driver not to kill you is also at odds with their knowledge that should they slam on the brakes to save you they run the risk of a pile up behind them.

Most drivers will run the risk to their own safety and slam on the brakes. But because the calculus required to assess the situation is itself difficult, in most cases their reaction will be too late to save your life.

That's a good analogy of an uncaring system. While it cares about human life in general it does not care about your life, or mine. If we try to cross six lanes of traffic without some assistance by the system (in the form of a handy walkway) or some cooperation from the drivers who use it we will surely die.

If we use this example as a metaphor for life as a whole with getting to the other side as one of our goals, then it is up to us to devise the best way possible to do what we need to do with the least possible friction. We don't want to die. We don't want to cause a pile up. We don't want the system to grind to a halt.

A certain amount of friction is inevitable within the workings of every system. This is why the world and its constructs and our personal constructs, never run smoothly. Friction is also inevitable every time one system crosses the path of another.

So, if the world appears chaotic to us, it mostly is. From our perspective. As a whole.

Being intentional requires us to chart a direction through all this perceived chaos that helps make sense of our journey. Why do we want to get to the other side of the freeway for instance? What are the required steps that will make this happen for us safely? What are we going to do after we get there? Why?

That's goals and direction. Intent and life journey, right there. Wrapped up in that example. I will finish off this section by paraphrasing Lewis Carroll's exchange between Alice and the Cat in *Alice in Wonderland*: If you don't know where you're going, any road will get you there.

How To Set Goals That Will Work For You

Setting goals and achieving them is what creates direction. Direction provides purpose. But purpose also affects the direction you will take in life.

If achieving goals is crucial, why don't we all succeed at achieving what we set out to do? The answer to this is that a lot of goals are unrealistic. We fall victims to the planning fallacy where we underestimate the difficulty and complexity of a problem (i.e. the goal we set ourselves to achieve) and then the Dunning-Kruger Effect kicks in and we overestimate our own ability to complete that goal. Not everyone suffers from these two biases however and a lot more people fail to achieve their goals than the opposite. Why?

A common problem is lack of focus. This is not the same as not working hard at something. I know a lot of people who work extremely hard and still fail to get anywhere. The problem is not their work ethic but the way they concentrate the output of their work.

Imagine I give you a pick. I tell you to dig the deepest hole you can in a given time. That's your goal. Now imagine I also tell you others are digging holes similar to yours and if you finish first, you will also get a prize.

You get to work digging at the ground.

Where I asked you to dig the ground is rock hard. You start off OK, highly motivated but half an hour later with your arms aching and your back covered in sweat you have little to show except a shallow indentation on the ground.

You decide to leave that spot and move further down hoping the ground is a little softer. Sure enough, you manage to make some quick gains there immediately but after about a dozen hefty swings the business end of your pick strikes rock. You're now stuck swinging at the ground but making no perceptible progress. You persevere of course because you're not a quitter. Neither do you shirk hard work. But after twenty minutes of swinging it becomes apparent to you that you won't manage to get through this rock to dig deep enough, quickly. You abandon this dig site too.

Your next effort is more successful. The ground is hard but chipping at it allows you to make some inroads. There is no rock but progress is achingly slow and you're running out of energy fast. By the time I come round again to see where you are you have a few shallow dig holes to show for all your efforts and one hole which looks like a decent hole in the ground but is nowhere near good enough to win you anything. You're now out of time.

What happened here? Clearly a lot of work was done. The fatigue you feel in your body and the shallow dig holes all around you are clear evidence of a massive effort to dig. But you still failed. You failed because you underestimated the difficulty of the task. You didn't put in place any appraisal mechanism so one place to dig, for you, was as good as any other place. You allowed action to take place before planning and thinking. As a result you wasted your time and strength and when you finally did have a chance you were too tired to actually dig a hole that might have got you a prize because you were out of both physical resources (i.e. you were tired) and time.

You may have been focused on digging, a.k.a. the action you undertook, but weren't focused on actually digging the deepest hole possible in the allocated time, a.k.a. the goal. Focus is about how to pick what's important so you can prioritize activities to make sense. The steps are simple: Create a plan that will actually deliver results. Then, act on it.

Don't dig holes in the ground that lead to nowhere.

Too many of us choose to grab the pick and dig in a race against time instead of actually taking the time to plan our action so we can get the best returns from what we do. If we were investing money instead of time and energy our approach would have bankrupted us a long time ago. Because we invest time and energy which seems to get replenished automatically as we go to sleep each night and wake up fresh, the next morning we tend to think we have a plentiful supply of both. So, we never take the time to critically examine the results we get, to think about why we do not get where we need to get to until it is too late.

The problem here is fundamental: we misidentify the critical resource at our disposal.

When we run out of money, we've run out of the ability to make investments in business. When we run out of time and energy, we are dead. Or as good as.

This final section of this chapter will help you understand what you need to do before that happens.

In the 1981 issue of *Management Review* appeared a mnemonic that will stay with you long after you've read the last chapter of this book: Work SMART not hard. SMART workers set goals that are:

- S = Specific
- M = Measurable
- A = Attainable
- R = Relevant
- T = Time-bound

If you had applied that strategy to your digging you would have ended up with a hole a lot bigger, much faster than what you did end up with.

Remember a couple of things: First, that goals that don't get you towards where you need to go are distractions. They need to either be cut out immediately or prioritized towards the very bottom of your list. Second, start with the end result first. Then work out how to get there.

The problem with your digging was that you focused on your ability and willingness to dig. Not the end result you needed to achieve. As a result you became distracted. You made mistakes that took time for you to realize. You wasted energy and time.

Treat your time like you're paying for every second you have. Treat your energy like it costs you money to renew every day. The moment you realize just how precious your time and energy really are you become more selective on where to allocate them and when.

That's the key to focus and attention. It's the key to how to better prioritize and how to create goals you can stick to that will deliver what you need.

Points to Remember
- Each person is a system.
- Friction is an inherent property of every system.
- Goals create direction. Direction creates purpose. Purpose closes the loop, refining our direction and changing the goals. This only happens if our goals are aligned to our purpose.

Question Time
- What do you think is your purpose in life?
- Do your goals in life align with your purpose?
- Do you have a clear idea where you want to be five years from now?

Top Tip
- Create a list of all the things that soak up time and energy for you each day. Work to eliminate at least half from that list.

4. Motivation

Motivation is the dirty word in most walks of life. When it's mentioned it's usually in the context of "you don't have it" or at least, you don't have enough of it and you need to somehow get it. People who fail to succeed are deemed to lack motivation. People who do succeed are considered to have some kind of secret formula that helps them get motivated and then stay that way.

When we don't understand something, we make up all sorts of things about it. Because we don't truly know how it works, we can ascribe all sorts of perishable or magical attributes to it. Before you laugh, remember that every time you touch wood to ward off bad luck, while surrounded by the high-tech fruits of 21st century technology, you too exhibit this approach.

Wood was sacred in the ancient world for its ability to float on water and burn in fires. It was vital for building shelters against the elements, keeping oneself warm, and as a raw material for tools, implements and amulets. To the minds of the people, it was both alive and dead, it could grow out of the ground and attain great size, but its death did not diminish it. By touching wood then, they evoked the life-force of the spirit that lived in it.

What has that got to do with motivation? Wood was tangible. It could be picked up examined, cut open, probed, and experimented with. And still we thought it was magical. Motivation is something that exists inside someone else. Most times we fail to understand it in our own self. We have no chance of really getting how it works inside another human being.

Or, at least that's how it was until very recently.

Let's bust the first myth first before we go on to shed light on the darkness surrounding motivation: Everyone's motivated. If they weren't we'd be surrounded by people who simply stood still, waiting to die.

Now, here's a simple truth: Everyone's motivated in a different way. This means that everyone's motivation is different. And that's where things get complicated.

So, let's unpack the complexity to get a better handle on this.

The American Psychological Association defines motivation as: "the impetus that gives purpose or direction to behavior and operates in humans at a conscious or unconscious level". Basically, whether we are aware of it or not, our motivation always makes us do something and, most times, it makes us continue to do something.

The beach body diet you undertake before summer hits, for instance, is initiated and then maintained by your motivation to look great on the beach, in summer. This is not just because you want to look and feel healthy by shedding a few extra pounds. It is also guided by your idea of how you should look in order to be thought of as attractive (a social construct), how you should look in order to elicit the admiration of others about your physique (social status and identity), how you should look in order to feel good about yourself and the way you fit in the external world (mental modelling and values) and how you should look in order to satisfy your need to attract a potential mate (basic drives).

All of these things are contained in the box that's neatly labelled "motivation".

Some of the things we experience that make us motivated to do something are conscious and subject to analysis. We know, for instance, the approximate date when we will be required to bare most of our body on the beach. We are aware of the potential for negative judgement if we turn up being overweight and looking unfit. We are probably painfully aware of all the many advertised products and services that will help us look slimmer and fitter. And we still, mostly, and usually make the decision to get ready a little later than we should.

This is conscious motivation.

If we were questioned about all this. If we were, for example, asked to place our hand on a tome that represents some holy scripture for us and swear in the eyes of a deity and before the legal authority of a court that could punish us, should we lie. And then the presiding officer of that court, demanded that we explain why we decided to reduce carbs and increase our level of daily physical activity in a particular month of the year, we will have no problem breaking everything down to the last detail.

We'd be able to talk at depth, why we are not quite happy with our physical appearance. Why there is a lot of social pressure to possess a physique and looks that fall within an acceptable range. We'd be able to talk about the unfairness of this but also of the necessity to conform.

Our analysis would cover facts about societal expectations and cultural structures. We'd talk about the practicalities driving global multibillion dollar businesses that lead to advertising that sells products and services that will help us look better in a beach environment.

The point is that all of the things and the reasons that drove us to act in a particular way would be transparent and accessible to us.

Knowing something. Being able to conceptually grasp it, does not make it any easier to resist. Especially if that something is part of the cultural tapestry of our life.

I am aware of the need to cut to the chase and talk about being intentional in a way that includes motivation but in order for it to make enough sense to be of practical use, I need to cover unconscious and subconscious motivation first. There is a difference between the two. Unconscious motivation is automatic. Your hand being snatched back from an open flame is a good example of that. Subconscious motivation is hidden from us, but it can be revealed if we care to think about it analytically. My fear of swimming in deep, opaque waters, in the Med, where the bottom of the sea is hidden from me stems from my childhood growing up in Australia at a time when the annual tally of shark attacks made headlines in my local Brisbane paper in Queensland.

This was not always obvious to me. It took a lot of soul searching for me to try and understand why I never ventured beyond the point where I could see the bottom of the sea unless I was on a raft of some kind, even though I am a really good swimmer.

In retrospect this is obvious. And it is obvious to you as I tell you. Yet that fact that it took a lot of thought and many tries for me to get to it highlights another truth: we all lie, and we all lie best to our own self.

In my case I didn't want to admit I was afraid. Despite it being such an inconsequential thing to admit and the basis for my fear had a deep logic to it, I engaged in spectacular mental gymnastics to navigate situations where I'd be in the water with friends and the bottom wouldn't be visible.

Go back up this chapter and look at the things contained in the box labelled "motivation" and you will see that even this small, inconsequential situation of mine exhibits all of those. To make matters worse the box that's labelled "motivation" is gift-wrapped in wide, strong ribbon that goes by the name of emotion.

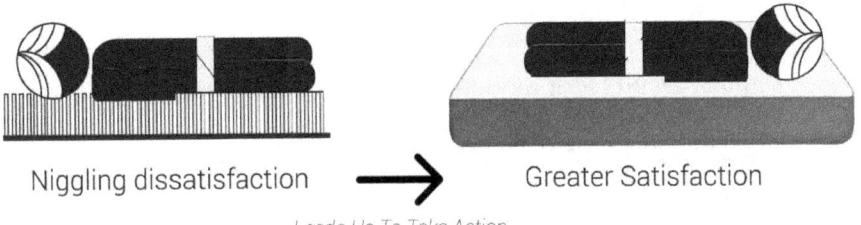

Fig. 4-1. Our motivation always flows in the same way: we go from a state of niggling and persistent dissatisfaction towards one where we feel more satisfied.

Emotion is what drives us. Unless we can truly feel something, we are unlikely to take any action at all. If emotions drive us, they also blind us. Avoiding being blinded without losing the drive we feel requires us to regulate our emotions. Acknowledge them. And then respond in a manner that is neither impulsive, nor robotic. Defining that fine line is what gives us real purpose. A sense of purpose makes us unstoppable because it takes our attention away from our sense of fallibility. This allows our intrinsic motivation to emerge.

The Things We See And The Things We Don't

Unfortunately, when it comes to understanding ourselves nothing is simple.

So, let's start by saying that it's not just our conscious thoughts that guide us. Our subconscious self too, plays a key part here. It is worrisome then that subconsciously (and even unconsciously) we can choose to, even more easily, give up the fight and go along with whatever appears to be the easiest option to us.

Consider that irrespective of whether our motivation comes from conscious, subconscious or unconscious triggers, its neural pathway is always the same. The brain, for all its complexity, doesn't have redundant circuits or duplicate pathways that act upon the same kind of action depending on its trigger. As far as action is concerned motivation is motivation, by whatever name.

So, regardless if the source of our motivation is visible to us and subject to analysis, its overall direction is always the same: We act to go from a place of niggling and persistent dissatisfaction to a place of satisfaction. This is true even if the satisfaction we experience is only relative and it results in a reduction in the overall level of dissatisfaction we originally experienced.

It does not matter if the origin of our dissatisfaction is hidden to us (subconscious or even unconscious) or if it is readily available even to a cursory level of analysis (conscious). The moment it reaches a point that is beyond our tolerance levels we will be compelled to take action.

This moment is also crucial to understand. Neuroscientific research involving fMRI analysis shows that the moment the critical threshold of dissatisfaction is reached in the brain specific neurochemical messengers accumulate that make it inevitable that neurons are activated and axons, the threadlike, portion of a nerve cell that carries nerve impulses away from the cell body, fire.

The firing of an axon is not unlike a lightning bolt. It requires the accumulation of a positively charged ion environment that takes place inside the neurons and the discharge of an electrical impulse that sends a bolt of electricity along the axons, which in turn activate other neurons.

The moment the cells decide to fire there is no stopping them and there is no halfway house response. Cells either fire or don't. Axons are either activated or they are not. When they are activated and fire they are activated fully. This is called the all-or-none law.

All this happens inside our head. In the real world, outside, we are motivated to take action.

I have simplified the mechanism of this process because this isn't a book about the complexity of our neurochemical make-up. What we need to understand is where our motivation comes from and why it is impossible to stop ourselves when we have made the decision to take action.

To complicate matters even further our body's and mind's decision to act predates, by a significant amount, our conscious awareness of our decision to act. This means that the choices we feel we consciously make are made for us by the accumulating load of dissatisfaction that reaches a certain threshold. When that threshold is reached the action we need to take becomes inevitable. We can no longer control it than we can control the inevitable snatching of our hand from the touch of a naked flame.

The Motivation Pendulum

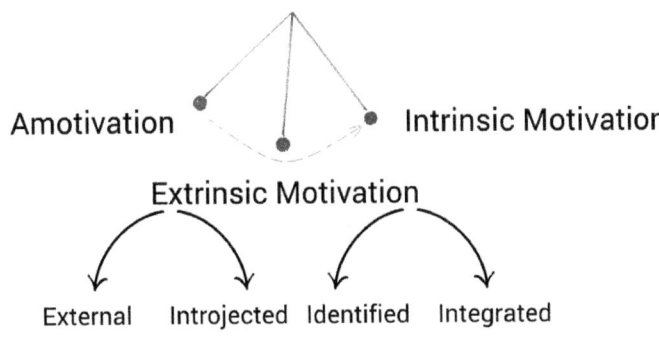

Fig. 4-2. *The motivation pendulum shows how our moods and feelings oscillate according to our experience of a variety of external stimuli and internal factors.*

If our actions are the result of the direction of our state of being from dissatisfaction to satisfaction, the moods we feel are directly linked to our motivation. Our motivation, in turn, swings between compete lack (i.e. a state of amotivation or apathy) and a state of complete intrinsic motivation (i.e. great internal satisfaction). This is called the motivation pendulum.

The key question to all this is: can we control our motivation? Can we guide it even? The answer is not quite as straightforward or even as full of hope as I'd like it to be, but it is less grim than you might expect it to be.

How We Learn And What We Learn

It is tempting to see life as a series of choices. When we string them along and look back we have a picture of its course. Its twists, turns and even ups and down then become obvious. It may also seem to us, in retrospect, that the choices we made, the decisions we took were almost inevitable given the circumstances.

The picture that emerges when we take stock of our past, this way, is one of navigating an unruly sea in cockleshell boat. Life, we think, is something that happens. We experience its effects. We react to its impact upon us. We get caught up in its ebbs and surges. Its events catch us unawares.

This is not how it is.

Suppose we change the visual imagery I just used. Let's look at life as a movie with our self as its protagonist. We write the script, we choose all the main plot twists. We ride out the challenges thrown up by limitations in the acting ability of our support cast, or the lack of backing from the executive producers or the external complications that arise out of the timing of our theatre release because of other movies or the state of the economy or the weather.

How different is this picture now? Even if the events we experience are exactly the same the sense we get over who makes the choices, who is in control is completely different.

In the first image I used of a massive, unruly sea and our tiny, fragile boat in it with us navigating we feel small and helpless. Unable to control anything our role is reduced to trying desperately to survive by picking the path of least danger to us.

In the second image however, as protagonists, the starring role not only places us in control of our own destiny, it also gives us the opportunity to create drama that spices up the plotline and makes us feel truly important to its development arc.

A smart critic here will say that this is sophistry. I am using specific imagery that is itself clearly defined by its limitations and applying it to something as fluid, uncertain and seemingly uncontrollable as life. But that's not what I am doing here. If we consider that in either setting there are choices we will make that we are not truly conscious of and paths that we will take before we are fully aware of them, what really changes is our perception of what we do. Our innate understanding of our role.

Neuroscientific studies have shown, time and again, that perception, our understanding of our role in particular contexts is backed by a cascade of hormonal states in us that change our physical, mental, emotional and psychological make up. This is the classic "is the glass half-full, or half-empty?" question. But upon the answer depends what neurochemical states we experience. The neurochemical states that we experience, in turn, determine what neurobiological resources we can call upon.

Research shows that optimists live longer. They experience a lot less stress. They self-report measurably higher states of happiness and life satisfaction when compared to pessimists. They feel more in control of their choices and decision making. They believe they are in greater charge of their life. Their choices lead to actions that produce, overall, better outcomes.

Tellingly, they also experience less stress or rather, they experience the same stress as everyone else around them, but they are a lot more adept at managing it and, as a result, experience far fewer damaging physiological changes, such as heart disease, liver disease and gastrointestinal problems, that are routinely associated with unrelieved stress.

The way we view life then (and ourselves; living it) is crucial in how we respond to the challenges we encounter. But is there something we can do to actively take control from the very beginning? Is there a course of action that will allow us to feel that what we do and how we do it, our motivation basically, is something that we can direct to the extent that it becomes an extension of our will? In other words, intentional.

It turns out there is. Research carried out across university labs that look at the psychology of pessimism and the neuroscience of the brain when it labors under specific assumptions and beliefs; found that those with greater resilience and the ability to bounce back from setbacks held assumptions and beliefs about themselves and the world that allowed them to see things in a much more global perspective.

The way we learn, it turned out, is critical here. And while both optimists and pessimists are equally capable of learning from their situations and applying the lessons they take away to fresh scenarios, ahead, it is only the latter that consistently benefit and achieve better outcomes for themselves. The reason for that is because of the way optimists learn.

Basically, all of us have the same two cognitive mechanisms that help our brain learn. One allows us to learn from experience or by association. It relies on context and helps us create behavioral models that enable us to navigate each situation we encounter and future situations we encounter that are similar to what we have experienced directly. This is called social learning and it is a learning mechanism we have in common with countless other animals and insects that rely on social interaction to survive the threats posed by their environment.

The other learning mechanism relies on structured learning and reinforcement that take place in order to achieve specific long-term goals. This is called goal-orientated knowledge acquisition. It is unique to us, as humans, and it enables us to acquire and retain the knowledge and skills we need in order to become, at some point in our future, something different to what we are now.

The apprentice becomes the master this way. The student becomes the future doctor, architect and astronaut. The child becomes the adult self.

Most times, most of us employ both mechanisms depending on our particular situation and direction in life.

There is a catch, however. The brain uses different parts of it to store what we learn. When it comes to situational learning that's based upon experience the brain is willing to overwrite the memories it has in order to keep the most current ones.

This makes perfect sense from an energy-efficient point of view. It is highly unlikely that we can experience two different contexts and situations at the same time. Where we are, what we do, the culture we live in, the friends we keep, the job we have, the language we speak and the problems we experience as a result of all this are strictly local in time and space. To navigate them successfully the brain does what it is designed to do, it allocates resources to help us deal with them.

This is how we make it through a crisis, for instance. Or how we get through our day.

On the other hand, learning that has taken place with long-term goals in mind is stored in parts of the brain that are not given to being overwritten. Again, this makes sense. You don't want your driving skills, for instance, to be overwritten by your recently acquired bread-making ones just because you haven't driven for six months. Nor, do you want, everything you know about open-heart surgery to be overwritten by scuba diving, just because you took a sabbatical.

The brain's function that is designed to ensure that we can focus on dealing with our current situation without confusion or distraction and can acquire new knowledge and skills without forgetting the old ones we have, creates an issue when we fail to plan.

Without long-term goals that require the active acquisition of fresh knowledge and new skills we become trapped in the situational awareness of our current and ever-pressing circumstances. Without long-term goals that require us to conceptualize what we learn differently and store the memories of what we learn in long-term storage in our brain, we go from one day to the next, dealing with each situation we face as it arises, learning extraordinarily little that allows us to break out of that cycle.

We become, as a result, predictable, staid, unimaginative, and boring. Each day is a repeat of the day before it.

The easiest way to illustrate this is to use the imagery of a highly-trained, extremely well-equipped and very able platoon of soldiers hankering down behind fortifications in the middle of a raging battle. Without a plan, a strategy that provides a long-term objective, their entire focus is, understandably, on surviving the onslaught of the battle and staying alive.

This platoon of soldiers is so good that none of them dies in battle. Yet each day they wake up, check their weapons, and launch themselves upon the war that is taking place around them. Some days they may have a great win. On other days they may suffer some loss of some kind. But generally, nothing changes. Despite the fact that they all manage to survive, they fail to move forward. They don't truly understand the strategy of their enemy because they do not understand the enemy's long-term objectives. Because they lack long-term strategic objectives of their own, they fail to truly understand the meaning or importance of each win they achieve or each loss they suffer.

Their plan is to survive the day. Or survive the war. Because they have no other plan than that they are caught up in a hamster wheel of activity that is their daily grind.

Fail To Plan And You Do Plan To Fail

Despite what quotes shared across Facebook and the internet at large may claim, the adage "When you fail to prepare you prepare to fail" and its many variations that include the word "plan" did not originate with Benjamin Franklin. While its origin has probably been lost and is attributed, correctly, to anonymous sources, its first credible appearance in print is attributed to the Reverend H. K. Williams in 1919. He included it in the first edition of that year's volume of the religious journal *The Biblical World*.

I know this because in the pre-Covid world I used to criss-cross the globe giving presentations to business groups and corporation VPs and I had to research its provenance. That, knowledge acquisition was situational. It has stayed with me because I was able to transition it to knowledge acquired when studying Chemical Engineering. Benjamin Franklin who was a Founding Father of the United States of America also carried out a kite experiment that connected what was then known about electricity with lightning.

It's always amazed me how much the world of the present was shaped by polymaths in the past who were incessantly curious about the world and could transfer their knowledge of one domain to another.

This small, anecdotal example shows the ability to recall clearly and in detail information, however trivial, that is linked to knowledge acquired with long-term goals in mind. However, my choice of adage to cover here has another, far more important, aim. Planning involves what I call Future Gazing. Future Gazing allows us to project our self, mentally, into a future scenario which then gives us a direction to aim for and a series of actionable, incremental, and achievable steps that will take us there.

To use the example of our amazing Platoon of highly skilled soldiers who are caught in a hamster wheel of largely repeated, daily activity, if they could see themselves capturing the capital city of their enemy or destroying all of their enemy's supply depots, they would start each day engaging in the action required to incrementally take them to that goal.

The steps they would take each day would be different. Their calculus of risk and reward would be different. Their strategy would have a distinct direction and actionable steps. Their thinking would be different. Their mood would be different. And, as a result, their motivation would be different.

The war this amazing platoon of soldiers is in would be the same. The risks of each active contact with their enemy would be the same. The need to not get killed would be the same. Everything around them, in fact, would be the same. But because their motivation would be different, they'd be able to act in ways that would also produce, for them, the outcomes they need.

Future gazing allows us to see the future we want to exist in, so we can actively take steps to make it happen for us.

Planning long-term provides us with a sense of direction. It allows us to see the need for transformation. The need for transformation enables us to handle knowledge and skills differently. It makes us capable of conceptualizing. It activates neural pathways that store memories differently in our brain. We learn better, understand more. And, in the process, begin to also comprehend how our values manifest themselves in our actions. How our identity guides some of our choices.

In neuroscience and developmental psychology this is the basis of self-determination theory. Self-determination theory explains human motivation as a multi-factorial construct created out of our sense of who we are, what we are worth, what others think of us, how we feel about our self and how much control we think we have over our own life.

In its simplest form all that boils down to three elements: Competence, Autonomy and Connection or Relatedness.

In order for us to be intentional and our motivation to be under our control we need to have a clear understanding of the direction of our life and the purpose of that direction in relation to our desires. It's not enough to "survive the day". We can certainly do that, day after day, but without a strategy we fall into behavioral patterns of repetition.

Life then becomes a series of repeating cycles of activity that mark the passage of time as we age without our becoming wiser, wealthier, smarter or better in any sense. At some point life itself runs out.

Direct Your Motivation

We have seen already how to better understand who we are and how to set goals for our self. To direct our motivation, we need to ask a simple question: What would make us happier? An honest, realistic answer here, I suggest, would solve the issue for us.

In the case of my imaginary platoon of exemplary soldiers, the answer would say: "We want to win the war and go home." That answer would immediately help crystalise their goals and manifest the plan they need to make it happen.

So, if you find yourself caught in the hamster wheel of a daily grind where every day feels the same as any other day and the weeks turn into months and the months into years without much changing for yourself materially, mentally, or psychologically you will want to address the emotions you feel and dig deeper to discover your real desires.

What is it you want? Really?

How do you propose to get it?

What are the steps that will take you there?

What do you need to make those steps happen?

Answer all this and your life will start to change. You will change. Not because materially your environment will be any different but because perceptually you will become different. You will then find yourself making different use of what you have. Your calculus of risk and reward will change. You will make different choices, take different decisions and engage in different actions. And that will change the outcomes you receive.

Points to Remember

- We are always motivated to act. We are just not always motivated to act to achieve what we say we want to achieve.
- When we understand what makes us unhappy and can clearly articulate it, we are better situated to see what we need to do to make us happier.
- Planning is an activity that helps our goals match our purpose.
- Motivation is the result of clarity of purpose and certainty of direction in life.

Question Time

- Do you make plans that are detailed, clearly articulated and marked by realistic, attainable goals?
- Do you sometimes feel you have no motivation? Why do you feel that way?
- What is the one thing you would change for yourself after reading this chapter?

Top Tip

- Detail where you see yourself being a year from now. Then a year after that.

5. Behavior

If we always knew how to best behave in every situation, we encountered in our life we'd live a charmed life full of opportunity, great friends and much happiness. None of this happens to any of us. That's because none of us know how to best behave all the time and some of us probably manage to not know how to best behave most of the time.

That leads to miscommunication, issues, problems, misunderstandings, and conflicts. All of these then require additional mental, physical and emotional resources to resolve.

We don't know, cannot know, how to best behave in any given situation we encounter in our life for obvious reasons: life is unpredictable, and we cannot always be prepared in advance for every scenario that happens around us. This very real and very credible excuse is not however the "get out of jail free" card we may think it is.

As it happens there are ways to make sure that our behavior is better and our journey through life is smoother. Before we get to that however it's instructive to ask "why?". Why is it so hard to behave in ways that serve us better? Why are we so adept at creating problems for our self?

The Covid-19 pandemic answered both these questions.

During the pandemic, across both the digital and the real world, there was a marked increase of aggressive behavior. A United Nations' report commissioned as part of its "EVAW COVID-19 briefs" revealed that one in five women in the western world experienced aggression and sexual harassment. The percentage rose to almost half in countries like Pakistan where there is already an established patriarchal culture.

A UNICEF report, released at approximately the same time, polled 170,000 participants aged 18-24, across 30 countries and showed that at least a third of them had experienced online aggression and harassment.

In the real-world things also got worse. Beyond the many anecdotal instances many of you have probably encountered already, there are documented instances that quite literally take your breath away. A report published in the journal *Forensic Science International* showed that "In China, domestic violence is reported to have tripled during their shelter in-place mandate. Additionally, France has indicated a 30 % increase in domestic violence reports, Brazil estimates domestic violence reports have jumped 40–50 %," and the figures are similarly alarming across countries like Italy, Spain and the United Kingdom.

In the United Kingdom, in particular, the land whose public image is one of five o'clock tea, super-polite natives and a cultural emphasis on public decorum, a report released in 2020 cited that "assaults on Transport for London employees have risen by nearly 25 per cent in the past three years, from 505 to 628, while the RAC's 2019 *Motoring Report* found that 3 out of 10 drivers had witnessed physical abuse on the roads in the previous year, with the number of people whose single biggest fear was the aggressive behaviour from other drivers having doubled in 12 months."

Make no mistake, the Covid-19 pandemic is a stressor that eats up emotional resources, weakens or completely dissipates cognitive filters and removes restraints that allow us to maintain civility towards others. But the pandemic, though it is a contributory factor, is not the true, underlying reason for such an across-the-board increase in hostility towards fellow beings.

Tempting as it may be to see such widespread hostility as a disfunction, it is unfortunately, quite the opposite. The brain, in this case, functions exactly as it should and acts to protect us from a perceived threat. Faced with the actions of individuals we cannot understand completely and have, as a result, no reason to trust, the brain falls into patterns of analysis and interpretation that are described as hostile attribution bias. We see, in other words, attempts to harm us. We perceive a clear, to us, hostile intent in such attempts.

Such perception activates our fear response and its attendant binary choice of "fight" or "flight". Seeing how we cannot easily extricate our self from a screen or a real-world situation, or are not willing to, this leads to an expression of aggression as a manifestation of the "fight" response.

So far, so good. We understand what happens and what triggers it. But why does it happen? Really? Why are we so prepared to believe that a person we've never met is willing to act in a way that may harm us; which then predisposes us to acting badly towards them?

This is where the Covid-19 pandemic and its unforeseen consequences kick in. The global response to a pandemic that was highly contagious and quite dangerous, when there was no vaccination available was to social distance, wear masks in public and impose initial and sometimes repeating lockdowns that isolated us in our homes.

Despite the modern myth of rugged individualism and survival, itself a perverted and twisted misrepresentation of what was initially put forward in the famous Chicago address in 1893 by Harvard Historian Frederick Jackson Turner, we are no more capable of 'making it' on our own than we can survive in the desert without water.

The brain is the most complex organ in the universe. It requires a heavy input of information to function properly, and it calibrates its behavior through complex self-imposed filters that regulate emotions and behavior. These filters may be self-imposed, but they are formed through the brain's understanding of norms and its calculus of what is gained and lost when these norms are not followed.

Psychology calls this social cognition and describes it as: "…a sub-topic of various branches of psychology that focuses on how people process, store, and apply information about other people and social situations."

Social cognition, basically, allows us to understand how we should behave around other people. We could assume, wrongly, that being intentional means that we do whatever the heck we want. That would be OK if our sole purpose in life is to be wilful. But that is not going to make us happier, more productive or even help with our long-term survival strategy. For all of that we need other people or at least a degree of meaningful interaction with other people.

The global restrictions that were imposed as a means of dealing with the pandemic in its initial stages heavily impacted on our ability to interact meaningfully with others. Suddenly, finding a mate, keeping up with friends, even contact with family members became activities that were lost to us. We substituted this with social media in the online world, video conferencing, FaceTime, Netflix and even, thankfully, reading. But there were still times when we were alone.

The Lonely Brain

We are not born with many instincts. The instincts we are born with, however, in keeping with the purpose of instincts in all creatures serve the need to help us survive. They do that by enhancing our ability to cope with vital environmental emergencies. Humans have three basic instincts: self-preservation, finding a mate and social behavior.

A pretty strong argument could be made that during the Covid-19 pandemic restrictions and lockdowns across the globe the last one was severely circumscribed and, there was a majority of the global population for whom the last two were heavily impacted.

Our instinct for self-preservation allowed us to cope for a while. But not without side-effects. The rise in aggressive behavior, unfiltered social interactions, inappropriate social responses and generally poor decision making was not the result of the rise in perceived toxicity in newsfeeds or the use of social media or remote contact technology. All of this predated Covid-19 without our seeing a spike in anti-social behavior.

What we never had before this century was an experience of a restriction that starved our brain from the information it acquires during socializing in order to calibrate the norms within which it operates. The brain's operational parameters guide choices and decisions that result in our behavior.

Now that we have established that our need to 'belong', to be an active part in a wider, interactive community is a vital requirement for healthy brain function what can we understand about being intentional and the way we behave? Our behavior, in general, is guided by perceived explicit and implicit rules.

We crave rules because they provide certainty. We need certainty because it keeps our fear of the unknown at bay. We avoid the unknown because we are afraid of the risks it contains. We are unwilling to undertake risks we can't adequately calculate because we are unsure of the rewards. We are unsure of the rewards because we haven't quite worked out what we want and how to get it which means that until we figure out who we are and where we are going, we're stuck travelling in circles, through life.

A brain that's lonely is not just a brain that's bereft of the company of others. It is a brain that's starved of the information it needs to balance itself and function properly. This suggests that when it comes to behavior one approach we should take if we genuinely want to feel intentional, in control of who we are and how we evolve is to actively and by design seek the company of others. Try to socialize. Become involved in projects that have a community bias.

This is the first step. By choosing to put time, effort and energy in these activities we become responsible for the health (and balance) of our own brain. It seems easy but it is not. First of all, in order to prioritize friends, family, work tasks, goals and ambitions we need to clarify "who" we are and then the equally burning question of "why" we are.

If that sounds like we need to understand our purpose, it's because that's exactly what we must do. A sense of purpose is like a compass. It helps us keep true to our direction even when other distractions threaten to derail us.

At a neuroscientific level purpose is weird. Time and again research has shown that a sense of purpose, even one found within the context of a potential personal failure, can transform us. In his book on the subject, titled *The Invisible Leader* psychology lecturer and researcher Xach Mercurio recounts how in 2018, Desiree Linden, the first American woman to win the Boston Marathon in over 30 years almost gave up at the very start of it.

Linden, got really tired early on. In her post-race interview she said she was "feeling horrible" and experiencing so much pain from the race she was likely to drop out. Knowing that she was going to drop out she stopped thinking about getting a place in the race and she switched her attention on a fellow runner, Shalene Flanagan, who herself was struggling. Linden said she slowed down and talked to her, encouraging her and told her that "If you need anything—block the wind, adjust the pace maybe—let me know."

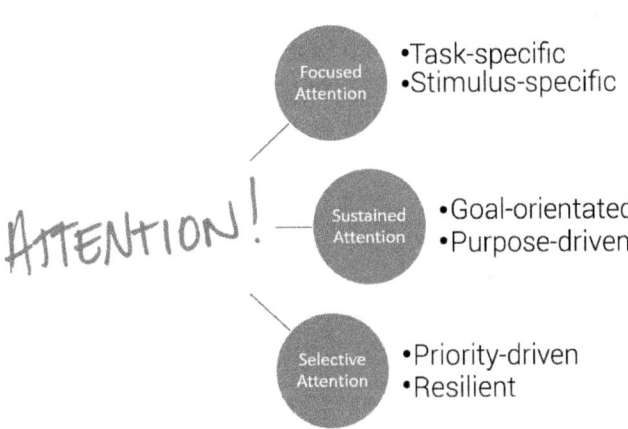

Fig. 5-1. Three Types of Attention: The division of our attention Focused, Sustained and Selective, allows us to become focused ourselves, passionate and resilient.

What is remarkable is that shortly after offering help to her fellow runner, Linden "got her legs back" and picked up the pace, finishing first in the gruelling race.

Helping someone without any expectation of reward or gain of any kind is motivated by a sense of our world view and our sense of self in that world view. It activates neural centers of our brain that are involved in empathy, compassion, and kindness. Studies carried out under laboratory conditions show that selfless acts of kindness release beta endorphins and neuropeptides in our bloodstream and both play a key role in pain management.

Did Linden's act of kindness made it possible for her brain to better manage the pain experienced by her body? If we take this point as our focus, we know that pain is highly subjective. It has a sensory component which is the strength of the signal sent from our body to our brain. And it has an emotional component which is our own interpretation of the strength of that signal.

What we focus on, personally, gets prioritized in our brain. Neurochemical resources are allocated to it. If we focus on the discomfort we feel, for instance, it gets prioritized. Anything prioritized appears to be augmented. Think how impatient you are to reach for a glass of water if you have been feeling thirsty on a hot day and have made the decision to pour yourself a tall, icy glass of water from the fridge. Suddenly your throat feels tight. Your hands are practically itching to get to it. You find yourself hurrying to the kitchen and, should the phone ring at that particular moment in time, you will most likely feel a hot burst of irritation flowing through you.

Yet, the water supply is plentiful. The kitchen is never far from the living room, even if you live in a mansion. And you are most definitely not dying of thirst. Focus, or "attentional direction" to use its more clinical term, have made getting that glass of water a priority. Suddenly we are painfully aware of how parched our throat is, how hot the day has become, how long it's been since we had anything to drink and how dire our situation is.

Running the Boston Marathon, Linden was feeling alone, in pain, and capable of focusing on nothing but the pain she felt. Running that race, at that stage, she was a lonely brain focused only on itself and acutely aware of its own ocean of misery. Quitting was a real option.

Then she stopped to help someone else. Her attention shifted direction. She became aware of other runners in a hard race, also struggling. She became attuned to them in case they needed help. The shift in attention most likely made a difference. As the pain receded to the back of her mind, who she was, the marathon runner she'd become, moved back to the center of her attention. The purpose of her had been redefined. Along with it so had her physical and mental capabilities.

Passion, Focus and Purpose

In an ideal world our actions, our behavior, would be guided by a clear sense of purpose. We need to feel we have some form of purpose because a strong sense of purpose becomes the foundation of the motivation we feel that leads us to engage in actions. As it happens purpose plays another, much deeper role in terms of what it does to our attention that is key to what happens to us and we shall get to that in a moment.

To clarify things, let's first determine the difference between motivation, which we've already examined in the previous chapter, and purpose. The American Psychological Association (APA), defines motivation as actions and behavior that have a clear will and a particular goal in sight while purpose is an object that's to be reached at some future moment in time. Breaking this down into plain English motivation is what we do to get what we need while purpose is the reason we do it.

In his book *Start With Why* author and speaker, Simom Sinek, says: "Your why is the purpose, cause or belief that inspires you."

Viktor Frankl, who survived the Nazi Concentration Camps, founded Logetherapy and authored *Man's Search For Meaning* believed that people are primarily driven by a "striving to find meaning in one's life."

Motivation is action. Purpose is meaning. Action without purpose has no meaning.

None of us, I think, lives in an ideal world so a lot of the time we experience moments or even long stretches of time when the purpose of our motivation is obscured from us. That doesn't mean we intuitively feel its push.

When we are not consciously aware of our purpose our motivation, our behavior is reactive. We react t because something happens which requires us to do what is required because we are motivated to determined by our motivation. Our motivation

79

total of our understanding of our self, our priorities in life, the general direction we head towards in our decisions and life choices, our values, our identity and our sense of belonging. These things are always in play. If we don't learn to actively own them, they own us.

Reactive motivation is still motivation. It will rarely take us where we want to go and it will not help us become fulfilled and happy in our life. Reactive motivation and reactive behavior surrender our ability to choose what we want out of life and the ability to achieve it, to the seemingly random set of circumstances each day throws at us.

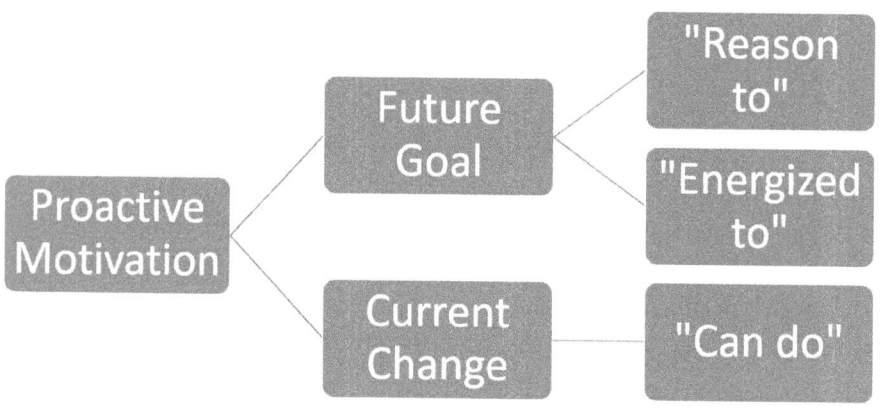

Fig. 5-2. Proactive Motivation leads to specific behaviors that are determined by our future goals and our current situation.

The opposite of reactive motivation is proactive motivation.

Industrial psychology researchers describe proactive motivation as "Being … about making things happen, anticipating and preventing problems, and seizing opportunities." They determine that it is made up of two dimensions, one being about future goals and the other about the current state of change that is required to happen in our self or in our general situation.

A lack of clarity in our approach in either of these dimensions will rob us of the motivation to achieve our future goals. If, for instance, our future goal is unclear or poorly thought through or unrealistic we not feel the "reason to" act sufficiently for our motivation to stay on will fail to act consistently with our future goal in mind. As a fail.

Similarly, if the change required in our self or our situation is too great, the implied energy cost required to achieve this change will seem large enough to stop us from taking the sustained action necessary to achieve our goal.

Proactive motivation then requires planning. Planning allows us to prioritize resources and direct our attention. Directed attention and prioritized resources make our behavior, intentional.

Being intentional in our behavior means we choose what to pay attention to. What we pay attention to is then chosen not out of whim but as part of a clear understanding of what we want to achieve in future. Our behavior, in this context, is what enables us to travel from the present us to the future us. It is what helps us navigate the complexity of the present without losing focus of what is key.

Inevitably, such directed, conscious way of behaving is sustainable only if we are engaged with the world, conscious of our actions and their impact and positive in our attitude. Passion that leads to engagement is, as it happens, part of the happiness equation we explore in the final chapter of this book. I won't jump the gun by exploring that aspect of it here but the components of passion that help us sustain a course of action that leads to a sense of greater purpose are worth mentioning.

The current psychological understanding of passion separates it into two distinct types that are known as the "Dualistic Model of Passion". One type is called Harmonious Passion. Harmonious passion originates from the autonomous internalisation of an activity we engage in. It leads to a coherent but less directed component of identity formation and it leads people to choose to engage in activities that they love. If you identify yourself as a runner, running frequently, for example, is part of your identity as well as the means through which you maintain your fitness. On days when you may be tired physically and be disinclined to run you may still choose to do so because of how you identify yourself.

The other type of passion is called Obsessive Passion. Obsessive passion originates from a controlled internalisation in identity, and it leads people to experience an uncontrollable urge to engage in the activity. Using the same example of seeing yourself as a runner, in a controlled internalization scenario, there are external pressures being applied such as social acceptance or internal ones like self-esteem. Often there is a combination of both external and internal pressures at work.

In this scenario not only do you see yourself as a runner, you also see yourself as a thin, runner. You need to be a thin runner in order to feel socially accepted as a person or in order to feel good about yourself so you run not for your health but because you feel you need to attain some externally imposed standard of beauty which will then allow you to feel OK with how you look. Obsessive passion controls the person who experiences it, and it leads to less desirable outcomes.

It is important to understand what drives us and why. The core difference to being intentional lies in choosing what to throw our weight behind instead of being thrown into 'the mix' by circumstances we don't quite understand and cannot control.

We will see what role focus plays here and how resilience arises from our attitude and behavior but first a hack that cuts straight to the chase: We talk about motivation, willpower, focus, values, beliefs, aims, aspirations, perception, principles, ideals and purpose. Deep down, these are the 'tricks' we employ to justify to ourselves the calculus we use to determine the effort required in order to get a reward. We need all the dressing of these complex attributes because we forget why we do what we do or fail to understand it in the first instance.

I believe that in every book there is at least one passage that manages to sum up the core of it so that if you read nothing further you will take away something that will help transform you. In this book this is the passage: When it comes to understanding and then, optimizing our behavior the equation of success, the hack I promised, explains that everything we do in the form of thinking, planning, effort, labor, money and emotion in an activity should use less energy than we expect to get back as a form of reward, should it succeed.

$$\text{Energetic Cost of Activity} < \text{Reward}$$

Fig. 5-3. The equation of success can be applied to any endeavour.

This is not hard to understand. Think about walking as a recreation and fitness activity. It has an energetic cost that increases in direct proportion to the speed at which we walk. But for each of us there is a threshold that is determined by our unique combination of biomechanical facility, limb length, weight, muscle composition, aerobic capacity and cardiovascular fitness. The moment the energetic cost of walking gets past that threshold our body breaks into a jog. We transport ourselves a little faster that way but the key element here is that the moment we transition from walking at our fastest possible pace to jogging the energetic cost of the activity drops. We are now in a new mode of transportation of our body. Its biomechanics are different to walking and though it may feel like more effort it actually uses up less energy than walking at our top available speed does.

This equation can be applied to everything: we get stronger muscles and leaner bodies because the exercise we engage in has a high energetic cost. The body then invests in building muscle (a calory expense) as an adaptation that allows us to exercise at a lower energetic cost. Startups burn through truckloads of money, passion and manhours but emerge with a structure that allows them to maintain their 'speed' and 'agility' in business and act as disruptors at a much lower energetic cost which then starts to deliver a profit.

Harmonious passion, for instance, allows us to optimize the energetic cost of our actions by aligning our values, goals and activities which, depending on what we do, creates a strong sense of purpose so that the energetic cost of action is decreased and the activity becomes sustainable. Obsessive passion is like a startup that never gets off the ground: it burns time, passion and manhours until they just run out or the startup itself gets disrupted and broken.

We can tackle running or other forms of exercise that way, doing them obsessively until we are injured or become ill due to exhaustion.

The equation of success is essentially an energy conservation one. As such it follows the laws of physics (thermodynamics to be a little more precise). It can guide our behavior, not by forcing us to always ask "what's in it for me?" at a crass, self-serving level but by revealing to us that effort reflects interest. Interest reveals attention. Attention signals priorities. Priorities establish importance. Importance reflects values. Values feed passion. Passion gives rise to purpose.

If we see ourselves as machines and apply this 'programming' to our operation, then we must understand that we are machines that feel and think in order to do. We need all those attributes to best apply the equation of success. In those instances when our thinking is muddled, our motivation uncertain and our actions confused we have not yet clarified what is important to us and why.

That's the role played by both focus and purpose. We need focus to cut out distractions; funnel our attention and get work done. We need a sense of purpose so we can maintain our focus, day after day on the things that will take us to a worthwhile future goal.

Resilience

From a 30,000ft perspective the history of the world is reduced to a few single-line observations. The 19th century was about industrialization. The world transitioned from a rural setting and cottage-industry economy to urban centers and factories. The 20th century was all about efficiencies of scale and optimization. Businesses learnt to be "lean and mean". Global supply chains were set up. Just-in-time production lines were created. The 21st century is about resilience.

That is also the general transition of the skillset and attitude of individuals living in each time.

The American Psychological Association defines resilience as "the process of adapting well in the face of adversity, trauma, tragedy, threats, or significant sources of stress."

Given the pandemic, and its aftermath, we've all experienced recently we could argue that "significant sources of stress" abound in the 21st century. How do we intentionally learn to be resilient?

The 21st century is full of uncertainty and challenges. The scale of the problems we face and their sheer unpredictability and complexity make it necessary for this to be the century we learn to build resilience in our systems and develop resilience in ourselves.

This begs the question of course: what form does resilience take? How do we recognize it in order to acknowledge it and take steps to develop it, if we don't possess it already? And if we do possess it already, how do we enhance it?

This is where neuroscience comes in and it starts its break down and analysis of resilience from the nuts and bolts: the way we respond, neurobiologically, to stress. Studies show that people who can go through stressful situations without suffering lasting psychological scarring have the capacity to sustainably exhibit the traits of mastery, commitment and competence.

A study recently published in the journal *Behavioral Medicine*, titled: *Adapting to Stress: Understanding the Neurobiology of Resilience*, had a particularly apt passage by the authors where they noted that:

"...active coping strategies, humor, hardiness, and extraversion can promote resilience through fostering feelings of mastery, commitment, and competence as well as the ability to help others through bonding. Importantly, the propensity of resilient individuals to express positive emotions, in relation to negative events, enables them to control their anxiety and fears."

When it comes to individuals these are traits that come under the broad and generally ill-defined label of 'character'. What is recognized to be character in an individual is usually called culture in an organization. The overlap between the two is virtually exact and it is made up of the same data points that define the dynamic of their trajectory; the direction of their path. A person's character guides his or her behaviour and the culture of an organization determines what choices it will make and what actions it will undertake.

Culture (and character) are guided by internal beliefs that form our perception and past experiences which then shape our expectations. In both, individuals and organizations resilience is then made up of the exact same three exhibited behaviors:

- Mastery
- Commitment
- Competence

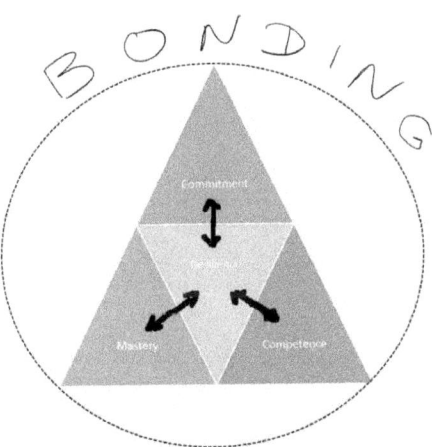

Fig. 5-4. Three behaviors of resilience that, incidentally, are also shared by many dedicated gamers.

The behaviour of cells when they encounter an environmental stressor is the perfect analogy of the behaviour of people when a company comes under stress itself.

What stops cells from running amok with neurochemically induced panic and paralyzing us with a cortisol overload is the person's ability to add perspective through perception and guidance through experience. Essentially, a person's ability to regulate emotions and apply guided reason in order to achieve specific outcomes. Take that into a company environment and you begin to see, I hope, the benefits to be derived by having a mission statement, corporate values and a real sense of purpose.

If a person's biology, essentially cells, play such a pivotal role in their behaviour what exactly are we looking for when we examine the differences in responses from people who experience extreme stress? To answer that question neuroscientist Richard Davidson from the Departments of Psychology and Psychiatry University of Wisconsin, used fMRI imaging to study brains under stress.

What he found was that brains that possess more axons, the white matter that connects neurons in the brain and interconnects different brain regions with each other, can tune down specific regions that initially react to a stressor and take more reasoned action.

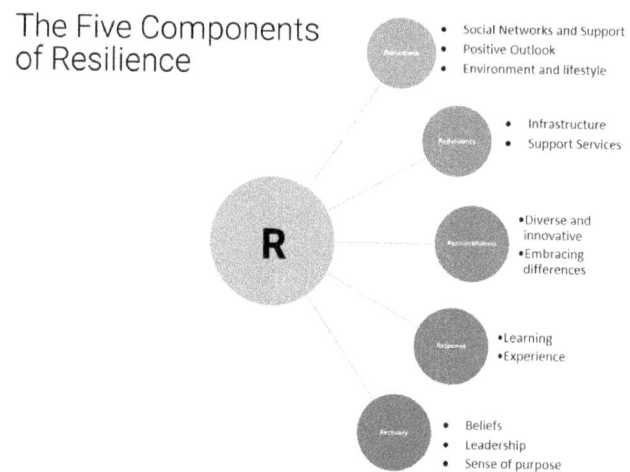

The Five Components of Resilience

- Social Networks and Support
- Positive Outlook
- Environment and lifestyle

- Infrastructure
- Support Services

- Diverse and innovative
- Embracing differences

- Learning
- Experience

- Beliefs
- Leadership
- Sense of purpose

Fig. 5-5. Attributes required for resilience.

A subsequent study published in the journal *Nature Neuroscience*, carried out by Eric Nestler of the Department of Neuroscience, Friedman Brain Institute, Mount Sinai School of Medicine, New York; concluded that the failure to be resilient in the face of adversity was a "failure of neuroplasticity". In other words a failure to adapt at a cellular level.

A 2010, detailed, study published in the *Journal Of Community Psychology* broke down the factors that resulted in rural Australian communities to be resilient and rebound from the experience of extreme adversity into twelve, very specific attributes, that stem from five distinct characteristics that define resilience.

The characteristics (and they're the same whether you're a person suffering a personal tragedy or an organization trying to rebound from an existential extinction event) are:

- Robustness
- Redundancy
- Resourcefulness
- Response
- Recovery

The attributes, from the Australian study, that map to these characteristics are: social networks and support; positive outlook; learning; early experiences; environment and lifestyle; infrastructure and support services; sense of purpose; diverse and innovative economy; embracing differences; beliefs; and leadership.

There are a couple of lessons we can learn from this, immediately. First, resilience is not something we can develop alone. It is a network effect that requires connection with others and their help and support. Second, the one unique component we bring to the table is our sense of purpose, the beliefs we hold and the perception we experience that is based on our past experiences.

As individuals we need to cultivate social ties, embrace social change and be public minded in our actions, in order to actively cultivate resilience.

Resilience, in turn, emerges as a direct result of our engagement with those around us; our engagement with the world.

There is one more element to all this that permeates everything we do. An element so fundamentally basic that it is remarkably easy to overlook. An element that, in a time of crisis, separates survivors from victors. An element that allows us to be resilient, be resourceful, be alert, be more than we think we can be when it most counts.

I could have explored that element in the previous chapter, when we looked at motivation, or in this chapter because it is part of behavior but in both these instances, while essential to both, would also have been a little ahead of its time.

To truly understand how we become intentional; how we seize control of our life and wrest its trajectory from the circumstantial jaws of the world, we need to comprehend, truly, the neurobiological impact of planning and preparation.

It is something we shall examine in the chapter ahead as we look at beliefs.

Points to Remember

- No one really knows how to behave.
- We need connection with other people to help us develop the social cognition necessary to guide our behavior.
- A sense of purpose acts as the moral compass that guides us in our choices and our actions when all else is uncertain.
- Kindness, empathy and compassion transform us both physically and mentally.
- Loneliness can unbind us.
- Motivation is action. Purpose is meaning.
- In a person, resilience stems from character. In an organization, it stems from culture.
- Resilience is a network effect. We need connection with others in order to develop it.
- There is a simple, effective and powerful equation of success you can apply to anything.

Question Time

- Can you name one instance in your life where you exhibited all five of the characteristics that define resilience?
- Which of the three exhibited behaviors of resilience do you need

to work on the most? Why?
- What is one thing you are most passionate about? How does this passion in your life affect your decision-making process and feature in the life choices you make?

Top Tip
- Go through your week and consciously engage in two distinct acts of kindness. When you do, reflect on how these two acts of kindness made you feel. Why?

6.   Beliefs

The Russian playwright and short story writer, Anton Chechov, famously said: "Man is what he believes." Now we know that from a neurochemical perspective and, inevitably, a biological one, he was right.

But how? And what does this mean for us, as people, who are brought up within specific sets of beliefs and, as we age, subscribe ourselves to other, specific belief systems? These are questions that are fundamental for our ability to live intentionally, direct our course in life, plan it, and reach specific goals along the way that allow us to feel that we have achieved our potential as human beings.

My journey to this book that maps our internal states to our external ones and vice versa and provides us with the means to better control our self, came by way of my last one *The Sniper Mind* that explored in detail, higher executive function and its role in critical decision making. That book came from my attention to semantic search and the way machines index and understand the external world.

It is somewhat ironic that we go back, full circle, into semantic search and then, by association, explore how the brain carries semantic conceptual representations which are used in the formulation of internal belief systems. We have to look at semantic search because the way an algorithmic spider collects information it finds across the web and takes it back to be indexed in a structured, relational database, is a vastly simplified representation of what the human brain does.

We don't have indexing spiders to send out but our brain constantly collects information about the outside world. That information comes from our senses and what we learn from others and what we can learn through our reading. The human animal is unique to all other animals on the planet in its ability to acquire information on and pass it on through books and songs and, in our days, YouTube videos and the web.

Education, in any form (and gossip is also a means of educating our self about the world) is a sensory stimulus that is divorced from its point of origin in time and space. A human being reading about a battle in history, watching a movie about life choices and the importance of having a family, listening to a song about the heartbreak of love and the difficulty of relationships, experiences the same activation of neurons inside the brain as if they'd been witnesses to the event.

We learn to be wise, brave, good and faithful to our mating partners, by creating internal models that represent scenarios that show us the consequences of being the opposite. That way we can learn to behave better without having to endure the consequences of behaving badly, which is probably just as well because we learn with difficulty.

The difficulty we experience in learning is not because we are bad at it, quite the contrary actually. Our brain is geared to learning and changing its structure as a result. We are capable of maintaining our mental sharpness throughout our life. But learning has an energetic cost. Evolutionary biology shows that our very survival hinges on our ability to conserve energy. We are therefore inclined to not engage in energetically costly activities unless there is a really good reason for it (i.e. survival in a "fight or flight" response).

Motivation, in this or almost every other context, is the reason we find to justify energetically costly activities. Consider that, in chapter four, I described motivation as going from a place (or state) of dissatisfaction to a place (or state) of satisfaction. Replace dissatisfaction with energetically costly state of being and satisfaction with energetically less costly state of being and you get the exact same thing.

How do then beliefs factor in this equation?

To understand that we need to understand what it is that beliefs actually do. A 2015 fMRI study of people presented with the same proposition proved that the brain of different individuals can light up differently and be interpreted by them differently even when they came from the same culture. Presented with the exact same indisputable facts people felt fear, hope, or desire. Beliefs then are a translator that tells us how we should feel about the reality we perceive. The way we feel drives our motivation and motivation is behind every observable behavior.

Beliefs are the backseat drivers of our behavior.

Embodied cognition purists might be inclined here to discount beliefs as an unnecessary complication and a remnant of the brain's older architecture. Beliefs, they believe, are hard-to-define entities that cloud the often direct way the body reacts to the environment. This is a kneejerk, and maybe understandable, reaction to the fact that beliefs can derail even the staunchest logician and frequently we find it hard to justify them. Things would certainly be simpler without them. By 'things' I mean the world. Yet, consider just how much we need beliefs to navigate the world. And, as it turns out, we need beliefs to enrich it.

Not all beliefs are equal however. Our internal belief system helps us navigate the world by interpreting the facts we observe and it determines acceptable ways to behave. This internal belief system that researchers often refer to as "guiding principles" is made up of three different types of beliefs: Experiential, Relational and Conceptual.

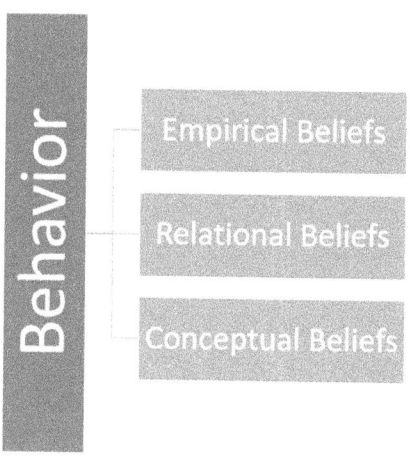

Fig 6-1. Much of our behavior derives from and is guided by our personal belief system. That system is made up of empirical, relational and conceptual beliefs. The makeup of these explains many behavioral differences we see between siblings who have experienced, initially, the same home environment and community members who are active in what is a commonly shared perceived culture.

Behavior, Beliefs and Mathematics

I am going to keep the mathematics part light on purpose in this section. Even at school, mathematics is an acquired taste for most people and most people fail to acquire it. So let's begin with behavior and let's start with a social experiment. In the pre-pandemic world this, admittedly, was a lot easier to carry out than in the present. As I am writing this book the pandemic is still raging so I have no idea what the "new reality" we are heading towards will be like.

Seeing, however, that human behavior has its own dynamic and exerts a largely irresistible force I am pretty confident that the 'crowd' of shoppers, holidaymakers or recreational walkers we were used to in the pre-pandemic world, will come back in some form. Now, for the experiment: walk through a crowd, any crowd of people and listen to the snippets of their conversations as they go by in twos and threes.

A single person, in a crowd, goes largely unnoticed. Everyone's attention is on their friends, the surroundings and whatever they will say next. They barely see, let alone notice, a single person going past them even if that person is heading towards them going the other way.

Here's what you will find: the majority of conversational snippets you will catch revolve around relationships. In particular behavior. Friends advising friends on how to approach someone they are interested in and what to say. People talking about people at work and how they behave in ways that irritate them. Some conversations revolve around bosses at work and their behavior and what to say and how. Some snippets are recounts of witnessed behavior by third parties that is held up for analysis. Others still are virtual monologues detailing a particular event and how the narrator behaved during it.

It will seem to you that the conversational subject that most engages, interests and animates the crowd is relationships with other people: romantic, platonic, neighborly or professional. You may catch the odd talk about diets or recipes or films or music, but at least six out of every ten snippets you overhear will be about behavior.

Now that I recount it here (and I often run this experiment in crowds when I am out and about alone) you may find it a little odd that so many people are talking about behavior. What is the real oddity however is that unless I mention it you are more likely than not to find it normal, because you also talk about this subject with your friends when you are hanging out with them.

Consider how crazy this sounds: despite growing up, working and living with people who speak the same language we do and share the same culture and have a broadly similar understanding of our surroundings, we still spend most of our waking time trying to figure out why they behave in particular ways and how we can behave in return. You can bet that the people around us also puzzle and fret over our own behavior and try to understand what exactly are our intentions, values and attitude so that they know how to behave towards us.

It is safe to say that with very few exceptions I shall touch upon in a minute, no one really understands other people, even those they are related to by blood or marriage. The exceptions are some people who are so deeply in love as to be in total tune with each other, twins, small groups of people engaged in initiating a project (startups, rock or pop groups), some but definitely not all sports teams and special services personnel. In these exceptions we can expect to come across the ability to say entire sentences with a nod and to convey deep meaning to another person with a glance.

This seemingly supernatural ability to communicate stems from an experience of boundaries. Boundaries (and love with its hyperfocus on another person to the exclusion of almost everything else, is a boundary) cut away the outside world, this limits the endless possibilities of context of social, personal and professional interactions. This, in turn, limits the interpretation and meaning we can ascribe to social signals, body language, words and tone of voice. By limiting the scope of our interaction with others we make it more engaging because we can allocate more attention to it.

Our powerful, human brain is designed to deal with social cues and body language and voice and tone and words and context. When we operate, however, within the constraints of clearly defined boundaries we can bring more mental bandwidth to bear and often find that the richness of the human experience only improves as a result.

We say more with less. Understand a lot with barely an explanation. The ever laconic Spartans declared war on the Persian empire, the world's first superpower with two words: Molon labe (transliterated from the Ancient Greek). The Victorians would dash complex, novel ideas and castigate entire cultures or ideologies by saying "I see."

Constraints add clarity even if they curtail breadth of vision. Clarity brings our values into sharp relief. Our values inform our beliefs. Beliefs guide our behavior. The road from our environment and its stimuli (both real and imagined) to our thoughts and deeds has never been clearer or more straightforward.

Yet, we still struggle to understand how we should behave. We struggle to understand the behavior of others. Mathematics is to blame here. If we model the trajectory arc of a relationship between two people who first meet it initially looks easy. Each person is associated with a number of variables that define them but the fact that neither knows the other creates specific boundaries framed by the unknown, that help clarify the initial stage of their acquaintance.

In that first instant it appears to be fairly easy to calculate what will happen next to this relationship, be it romantic, friendly or professional. Suppose we had a supercomputer at our disposal. We could imagine that all we need to do is input into it all the known facts and attributes of each person and then solve for the end goal of their intended aim. If, for instance, the aim is to end up with a romantic partner, in theory we should be able to determine with a high degree of accuracy whether that will happen and how it will work out.

This is not how relationships work however. We know from experience that the moment our two imaginary people step away from that first instance of acquaintance they broaden the boundaries of their common understanding of each other. This introduces fresh variables we need to take into account. At the same time neither of them is a fixed point in time.

The way each person in a relationship feels, within themselves, is also subject to constant and sometimes sudden change. Feelings, sensations, health, dreams and aspirations create a shifting backdrop against which what we call 'personality' and 'identity' are enacted. It becomes virtually impossible to predict the odds of a relationship making it because the initial conditions of its participants constantly fluctuate and the variables they will face at each stage of their projected journey are also in flux.

If we take as the initial meeting between two people the plot from *Pride & Prejudice*, we'd get the first critical point of data from the first meeting of Elizabeth Bennet with the dashing Mr Darcy at the assembly rooms where each formed an instant dislike of the other. But by the time they meet again at the ball at Netherfield where they share a dance and exchange more information we will have to contend with the additional variables of their respective interactions with George Wickham, Mr Bingley and Elizabeth's mother and sisters are introduced.

Each phase, each fresh layer of information, each interaction with supporting characters throws up fresh variables that need to be taken into account. For instance, the lack of decorum of Elizabeth Bennet's mother and youngest sister. The relative lack of means of her father and the family's precarious social position. The implied cruelty and callousness Mr Darcy showed towards the apparently gallant Mr Wickham. The intentions of Mr Bingley's sister towards Mr Darcy and the growing affection Mr Bingley is feeling towards the Bennet family.

The list goes on. It wouldn't deter us of course. After all we do have a supercomputer. We'd feed in all the fresh variables and then the variables after that and then the variables that each set of fresh variables introduces in turn. As we feed the information in our powerful supercomputer waiting for it to 'crunch the numbers' and spew out its prediction for their relationship, the witnessed nature of the relationship between the two would have changed.

The fact is that relationships are one of those activities where time broadens the boundaries and introduces fresh variables. Not only do the new variables present their own challenge as far as making the calculations goes, but they also force us to re-evaluate all the old variables that were in play prior to the point of introduction of the fresh data.

This leads to the interesting phenomenon that as the time of acquaintance between two people increases the variables introduced at each instance and the effect each one has on the next instance also increases. That means that the number of calculations required to predict a relationship at each point of its trajectory arc, also increases with each step. Even worse, the number of calculations needed to determine each point in this trajectory arc doesn't go down even if we use a 'better' algorithm than the one we started off with, each time.

In no time at all our number-crunching supercomputer will slow down and may even grind to a halt as it is forced to start recalculating from the beginning the odds of this couple's success to make it together through life.

In computational complexity theory a problem that requires significant resources to solve irrespective of what kind of algorithm is used to solve it, is called an NP-completeness problem, NPC for short. NP stands for nondeterministic polynomial time, and it's used for decision problem solving where parameters change over time. This makes the time required to solve the problem a problem in itself.

It is no accident that Pride and Prejudice a novel that's almost never stopped being a best-seller since its publication in 1813; a novel whose value and appeal is discovered afresh in each era, as the televised series and countless movie versions of Jane Austen's book, have shown, belongs to a genre called "a novel of manners".

The paradox with NP-problems is that the accuracy of any solution to them can be verified quickly, while the attempt to get to that solution takes such a large amount of time and effort as to render them unsolvable by brute calculations no matter how much power we throw at them. In plain English, a couple deciding whether to 'tie the knot' know pretty quickly just how well they are suited to each other.

Elizabeth Bennet and Mr Darcy decide quickly that their feelings towards each other have changed and they now like each other.

But for us, with our supercomputer, trying to calculate the odds of their relationship from the data we had in the first instance of their acquaintance is virtually impossible. We simply do not have sufficient time and each time we try we have to start from the beginning so we can include a fresh set of data and new variables.

Computer engineers working with NPC problems use a variety of techniques to get round them without bankrupting their organizations with expensive computer time. These involve the creation of heuristic functions and approximation algorithms that provide "good enough" solutions. Crucially when it comes to the "choosing the perfect mate" problem heuristic models and approximation algorithms also take a lot of time to create, test and calibrate. So, really their employment doesn't realistically solve this particular problem.

Yet, there are countless anecdotal instances where people who got together over a relatively trivial event, 'clicked' and stayed together through incredible difficulties in life. The problems they faced, rather than driving them apart, only served to bring them even closer together.

Decision-science research shows that a brain that's clearer in its sense of identity, purpose and values can make use of mental heuristics in its major decision-making moments. These are mental shortcuts created over time that pull together complex real-world knowledge to reach a judgement even when there is an insufficient amount of information for that judgement to be accurately made. The result is a "good enough" approximation that actually does the job.

The ability of the human brain to outstrip supercomputers in solving complex, real-world problems is showcased in the speed with which the brain recognizes what the eyes see. Using concepts and creating understanding out of the facts it sees, the brain can recognize an image the eyes see in just 13 milliseconds. The processing of visual imagery and the brain's computing power are so closely linked that solving for vision in computers almost simultaneously solves many of the problems associated with artificial intelligence.

To quantify the speed at which the human brain operates, two PhD students from the University of California, Berkeley, and Carnegie Mellon University have created a benchmark measuring human brain power against supercomputers using not the number of calculations per second but the ability to transfer information from one part of the brain (or the supercomputer) to another as the benchmark.

They called this "traversed edges per second" (TEPS) and showed in their study that when it comes to the transfer of information across the brain humans outstrip supercomputers by about thirty-to-one.

So, supercomputers may beat us, organic units, in linear calculation speed, but when it comes to making major decisions, we pretty much leave them standing. This is more than whimsy. We have even more concrete proof of this in the study of snipers and how their brains operate under pressure. Readers of my previous book *The Sniper Mind* which examined critical decision-making under pressure know that being able to adapt and overcome are the key attributes of trained snipers that enable them to behave in seemingly superhuman ways.

Tracking Point was an American company based in Austin, Texas that attempted to put in as much computing power as possible on the sniper rifle in an attempt to remove the human skillset from the picture.

Their premise was that the gun's 'brain' would carry out all the necessary calculations making the human firing it nothing more than a glorified delivery platform. The company has since closed down. Its guns required so much computing power that its price tag made it virtually impossible for any nation's military to buy.

Even more telling, despite the massive amount of sophisticated technology they'd packed onto the gun the best ever results they got were just 500m away. Compare that with trained snipers who can successfully hit a target that's 3,450m away. That's almost seven times as far with a virtually infinite number of fluctuating variable combinations that need to be taken into account.

There are two key takeaways from this. First, that relationships are really hard to do. Everyone struggles. We need all the help we can get (which is why *Pride & Prejudice* is still so popular) and no one can get them right all the time. The poor results of dating apps and match-making apps should have told us that already. The high rate of divorces and the number of times business partners fall out or music groups break up are simply an acknowledgement of this level of difficulty.

Second, by starting off from a different mental state than the 'average' we can load the dice in our favor and pull off amazing feats of mental calculations that will allow us to find our 'perfect' mate, clinch that business deal or make our own destiny with a band of like-minded, talented friends.

Intentionality, in this context, is beautifully defined by its neuroscientific definition: "goal-oriented behavior in which an individual uses strategies to achieve various ends or effects."

How do your beliefs, mine, those of the people around us factor into this? How do they guide our thoughts and change our behavior? The easiest example to use here as an illustration is to say imagine that you strongly believe that there should be no sex before marriage. Suddenly dating apps like Tinder that tend to incline towards the hook-up type of connection are off limits to you. Meeting someone at a party changes the entire dynamic of the exchange. The strategies you would now employ in order to get to the goal you want, i.e. to find a mate, will be entirely different.

Forewarned Means Forearmed

It is now more than fair to say that "Our beliefs become our reality. When we change our beliefs, we change our behavior." The quote is taken directly from a research paper studying the neurobiological effects of beliefs and the authors of the study included, in their review, the massive body of work done on the placebo effect where the belief in the efficacy of a potential cure produces measurable, verifiable, physiological effects.

The path that leads from a conceptual 'there' where we use labels borrowed from cognitive science to a 'here' that represents observable behavior is a chain whose links are made up of expectation, perception, reality and beliefs.

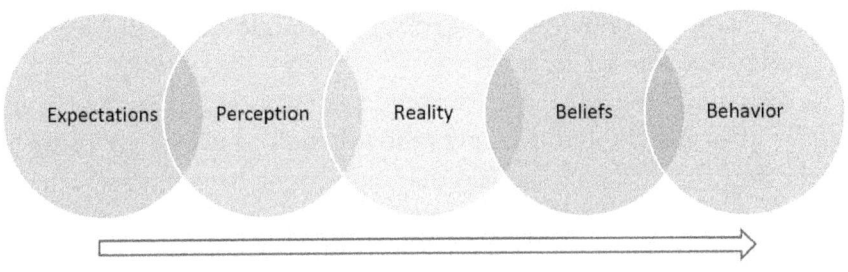

Fig. 6-2. Pathway from expectation to observable behavior.

Cognitive-behavioral models suggest that the beliefs and expectations individuals bring into relationships affect their thoughts, feelings, behaviors, and satisfaction in them. In turn this affects the evaluation of whether a relationship is 'working' and whether it has a 'future'. A study on relationships carried out by the department of psychology of Ohio State University and, subsequently published in the peer reviewed The Family Journal, found that its participants "expected their own relationship satisfaction, when dating, engaged, and married, to exceed their perception of the average American's; and participants expected their relationships to progress from dating through marriage with ever-increasing levels of satisfaction (an outcome contrary to what couples typically experience)."

Even if we are at a virginal state of sexual experience, we all enter a romantic relationship with expectations that arise out of prior experience. This experience has been learnt, in the first instance, through observation of family members, relatives, friends and later the wider culture through available films, songs and books.

Despite all this previous learning a relationship presents even experienced individuals with a host of unknown variables. The process in our brain that combines prior knowledge pulled from our stores of experience and uncertain evidence is known as a Bayesian integration. Neuroscientists at MIT have discovered distinctive brain signals that encode these prior beliefs. They have also found how the brain uses these signals to judge the decisions it's presented with, in the face of uncertainty.

This process can further trigger the brain's aversion to risk. In such cases it is outwardly expressed as racism, fear of the unknown and bias. But before we rush into a negative judgement here consider how this process, at the same time, prepares the brain to deal with the unexpected and survive it.

In their study the MIT team wanted to understand how the brain encodes prior beliefs, and then puts those beliefs to use in the control of behavior. The evidence showed that by running 'worst-case-scenarios' the brain prepares itself to quickly draw from all its available resources in order to guide behavior and deliver a positive outcome. Forewarned does mean being forearmed. Forearmed, as it happens, delivers vastly different results than being taken by surprise.

What is remarkable here is that the MIT study that took place in 2019 provided the neuroscientific framework for experiential and largely anecdotal evidence from the past. In particular it explains the efficacy of the late U.S. Marine John Dean Cooper color code. In *The Sniper Mind* I detailed in depth how John Dean Cooper who saw active action both in the Pacific theatre during world war II and the Korean War believed that in a combat situation survival has nothing to do with the weapon or the skill of the person. Instead, it hinges on their mental attitude, which he called the combat mindset, and their ability to quickly identify a situation and prepare themselves mentally, to meet it.

John Cooper went on to create the modern technique of handgun shooting but he also created a color code of preparedness that is the basis of how to think in a combat situation. Cooper's code, as it's popularly known, is still in use today. In a 2005 article he wrote he explained it like this:

> *"White you are unprepared and unready to take lethal action. If you are attacked in White you will probably die unless your adversary is totally inept.*

> *In Yellow you bring yourself to the understanding that your life may be in danger and that you may have to do something about it.*

> *In Orange you have determined upon a specific adversary and are prepared to take action which may result in his death, but you are not in a lethal mode.*

> *In Red you are in a lethal mode and will shoot if circumstances warrant."*

I am a firm believer in the instructive value of instances drawn from active combat scenarios. On the battlefield the margin for error is so small and the consequences of getting things wrong are so grave that the lessons drawn from them tend to be truer than anything else learnt in any other scenario.

Cooper survived bitter hand-to-hand combat situations and saw first-hand how mental attitude translates into survival. What we learn from his experience and the current research in relationships is that beliefs program us to behave in a particular way by preparing the brain to do so, in advance.

To better help you understand how his color code system teaches the brain to think in a combat situation I will run with you a highly modified version of the Gergen's Dark Room Experiment that I employ with my audiences across the world as an international speaker.

"Imagine," I say "that you are in your favorite room in your house. Visualize it with your eyes open, see yourself in it. Experience the sense of safety and peace you know when you are there, for a minute. The way you feel, during this brief amount of time, is represented by the white color in Cooper's color code.

I next ask my audience to close their eyes. "The lights have now gone out and you're in total darkness," I say. There is no immediate sense of alarm but any blackout in your house is a small cause for concern. Potentially something is wrong. Potentially it could affect you. Though, at present, there is no direct evidence to tell you so either way. You may feel a little bit worried but you're not overtly so and you most probably tell yourself not to be silly, and just stay calm. That, is the yellow color in Cooper's color code.

Next I say, "You're magically transported to another completely darkened room in some other house." Again, you can't see a thing. There is total darkness plus the sense that you're no longer at home which means your safety can no longer be taken for granted. Your senses here are heightened. Your heart rate and breathing have increased. You are aware of the nuance of sound in the darkness. You realize that you will need to be ready for anything because there is no guarantee that you're not in danger. You feel your body temperature rise. The first flush of anxiety in the butterflies in your stomach as your body prepares for either flight or fight. This now is the orange color in Cooper's color code and it's designed to prepare you to react to whatever may come out of the darkness at you.

Finally I add a clarification: "The room is occupied by someone who means you harm." At this stage the pounding of your heart in your ears drops significantly. Your hearing works overtime to pick up the slightest sound in the room. You find yourself working out survival strategies in your head. You may be quietly feeling about you looking for something you can use as a shield or a weapon. Your feet are making tiny motions searching out the topography of the floor that's hidden from your vision by the total darkness. This represents red in Cooper's color code.

At this point I usually have to ask my audience to finally open their eyes and practice taking a few deep breaths and holding them as I talk them down from their heightened state of readiness. Some of them get so drawn into this visualization exercise that they open and clench their fists and, occasionally, grind their teeth and clench their jaws.

There are two vivid lessons that can be drawn from my informal social experiment. First, we can all be so easily drawn into this experiment and experience its strong physiological and psychological impact because it feeds into our belief that the world is so inherently dangerous that a situation such as the one I describe in my final instruction is immediately recognizable as a threat. This elicits an immediate psychological response that's closely attended by a physiological one.

Second, the brain allocates emotional and psychological resources and triggers physiological ones in direct response to its understanding of the context of its situation. When I first start off this visualization no one in the audience appears to be worried or even disturbed in the slightest. When we get to the second stage there is a little bit of consternation perhaps in having to shut their eyes while sitting in a public space but that too is not really great cause for concern and I can see by their reactions that the visualization exercise draws so much of their attention that they don't have a lot of time to feel worried.

Things change drastically in stages three and four. For a start the focus on our internal state; our breathing, the beating of our heart, the temperature of the room we can feel, the feeling of the seat we are in against our body, all this disappears. The sensations, to be precise, are still there. It's just that the brain no longer allocates a lot of attention to them. Instead, the idea of a potential threat in the dark has our senses questing ahead. Straining to pick up data that can tell us whether we are truly in danger.

Cooper's color code is a basic belief system that tells us how to behave in particular situations so we can survive. Cooper saw time and again that those who were mentally and psychologically prepared for combat survived in situations were better armed or more capable comrades didn't.

The brain's ability to successfully deal with adversity rests upon its being able to adequately call upon specific neural centers. In a situation where the brain hasn't got time to do this, it panics. It recognizes that the body is in mortal danger. It shuts down the higher executive functions so they do not draw energy away from basic, reactive ones. It activates panic mode and tells the body "run or fight".

This is an evolutionary development that works to our favor when faced with a tiger or a hostile group of tribespeople from another tribe but it doesn't work so well in complex, nuanced environments like a modern battlefield or a boardroom.

Forewarned doesn't only mean forearmed. It also means that since we've been forewarned we know how to best behave. It also means that beliefs, like behavioral patterns, can be changed, adapted, modified or abandoned. How though? How is it possible to change our beliefs without, at the same time, doing serious harm to our self by weakening our sense of identity and challenging the validity of our perception? How, in short, can we change our beliefs without compromising our ability to safely navigate the world?

My suggestion here is that by answering these questions we also develop a game plan for resilience and gain the ability to contemplate change and adversity without necessarily triggering the fight or flight response that often precedes a sense of panic and inadequacy in us.

Change Your Mind But Still Be You

Are you the same person you were when you were eighteen? Is your body? How about your brain? Do you still have the same beliefs? More important to us still: do the beliefs you have guide you or have you accumulated the beliefs you need to guide yourself? The last question in particular can be restated as do we choose our beliefs or do they choose us? The answer to it determines the degree of cognitive autonomy we enjoy, the sense of agency we develop and the degree of freedom we have, to plot our own course through life.

The subtext of this section in the chapter, inevitably perhaps, raises questions about religion. Do you choose to believe in the deity you believe in or is your belief in a deity fostered upon you by neurobiology and evolution? To understand the even deeper implications of intentionality raised by this briefly consider the case of Khalid Sheikh Mohammed, a Pakistani imprisoned in Guantanamo Bay under the charge of being "the chief architect of the 9/11 attack on the World Trade Center" in 2001.

If we accept that he chose his beliefs then we also imply that he chose to believe he was on a mission from God when he planned the 9/11 attack he is accused of planning, and that he could have chosen to believe otherwise. This also raises issues about the alleged use of indoctrination in the spreading of extremism and the training of suicide bombers. But if we accept that his beliefs chose him and that he had no control over them we then must also accept that we cannot hold people responsible for something they have no control over.

I am not going to gloss over the fact that if the latter hypothesis is true then the entire point of this book is negated. However, since you're still reading and you're not even halfway through, you know that there is a way to reconcile all of this without resorting to the magical or the metaphysical which cannot, either way, be proven.

To do this, we need to start from the ground up with the obvious question of why does the brain need to believe in the first instance?

Siding with Chechov's view of beliefs psychologists define the function of them as the brain's way of making sense of the world and its complexity. They see them as "mental representations of the ways our brains expect things in our environment to behave, and how things should be related to each other—the patterns our brain expects the world to conform to."

It's tempting to say: there, done. Beliefs depend upon patterns. Patterns convey meaning. The brain is, amongst other things, a pattern detecting machine. Neuroscience now has a considerable body of research data that shows how the human brain goes into hyperdrive mode the moment it detects a pattern in the information it has been presented with.

Pattern recognition is a key element of learning and decision-making. The temptation to say I am done here stems from the fact that we can so easily now connect data, patterns and beliefs. Any belief that cannot rest on a pattern that's been detected within the data that has been presented is patently a false belief. False beliefs can then be discarded.

Unfortunately this is not how our pattern-detecting superpower works. The brain is wired to detect patterns in the information it is presented with because patterns are key to understanding what is happening in the world around us. That understanding enables us to take action long before the action we need to take is forced upon us by the environment.

A flock of birds taking flight, linked with rustling in the tall grass that doesn't follow the wind alerts us to a pride of lions coming down our way long before we have to rely on our puny strength and speed for survival. We're so hypersensitive to patterns however that we are predisposed to see them even when they don't exist. The flock of birds may have just finished their lunch and the movement of the tall grass may have another explanation. Because a wrong interpretation here will not kill us we survive and develop brains that do see patterns even where there are none to see.

The classic example here is the optical illusion of seeing a square where none has been drawn or seeing a Kanizsa triangle when none exists.

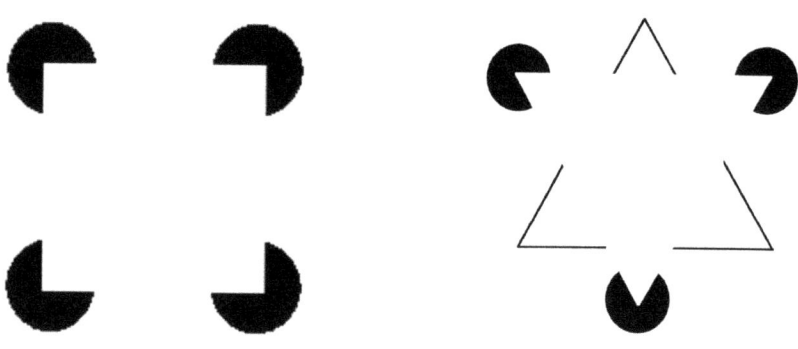

Fig. 6-3. The brain sees two triangles and four circles or a square and four circles arranged in an overlapping, 3-D construct when none of these images actually exists.

In figure 6-3 the brain sees, on the left, a square floating above four circles (known as pacmen, due to their shape) and occluding part of them with its edges. On the right it sees two triangles, inverted and superimposed upon each other. The topmost of the two also occludes part of four circles with its corners.

None of these figures exist except inside our brain. To construct these images out of the geometrical shapes that are placed on the page the brain carries out some insightful mental gymnastics. First it rejects coincidence. Because it acts on the belief that an arrangement of geometrical lines, like that is not likely to have been put there at random it ascribes meaning to them creating an elaborate three-dimensional construct with overlapping elements.

The Kanizsa triangle optical illusion is fascinating because of the way we process visual information to understand the world around us. There is a lot more, in-depth information about it in Appendix I at the back of the book. What is key for us to understand here is that our brain works the way it does because, from an evolutionary point of view, it has enabled us to survive.

By rejecting coincidence, it admits to itself that there has to be meaning in what it sees. It then interprets the data in a way that makes sense to it. There are two key points here we must consider. First, it is our belief system of how the world works that enables us to create meaning out of a meaningless, but purposely organized collection of lines and shapes. Second, since we've rejected coincidence as an explanation, we are now bound to engage in and accept an ever more elaborate explanation for what we perceive.

If, for instance, we never knew triangles existed we'd still be forced to invent an even more elaborate explanation for what we see. Our lack of knowledge wouldn't have been an obstacle in that regard. Consider how, very recently, in the real world the QAnon conspiracy took off. A paedophile, secret, global cabal intent on subjugating us all, suddenly doesn't appear that far-fetched an explanation for events that, we are sure, must have an explanation.

As an insightful aside on how we think, consider then that the first step to believing in a conspiracy theory is found in the brain's unwillingness to accept coincidence as an explanation for facts it observes. The brain is a meaning-making machine. Understanding what things, we observe mean has helped us survive. At the same time, we need to know enough to understand where the limits of meaning lie and when, sometimes, the things we observe are truly random. For that we need education and nuanced thinking, and both of these are attributes that need to be acquired.

This seems to provide a relatively easy solution to our conundrum. Educate yourself. Thing more analytically and you can then be able to change your beliefs without threatening your sense of who you are. That would also make it incredibly easy to be intentional. You, me, and everyone else who cares about this could just choose to cherry-pick whichever set of beliefs will deliver for us the outcomes we seek in order to best feel in control of our life.

The ease of this is an illusion. Beliefs and identity go hand-in-hand. What threatens one threatens the other. Anything that threatens our beliefs also challenges our assumptions (and the way we arrive at them) so our basic operational system also comes under attack. We're not hardwired to resist change in our beliefs but we are hardwired to survive. A challenge to the way we live our life and the sense of who we are is, quite rightly, perceived to be an existential threat. We'd go to war, figuratively and literally, the moment we experience it.

Geoff Heath, who used to be Principal Lecturer in Counselling and Human Relations, University of Derby, in the UK frames the whole beliefs and identity issue this way:

> *"We are not born with beliefs. Our beliefs are learned and become so embedded that we cease to be conscious of them. They become habits of thought, feeling and behaviour. We are not born with identities. We are what we come to believe ourselves to be. To change our beliefs is to change our identities. To have our beliefs challenged is to have our identities threatened. That's why it's difficult to change our beliefs. It's also why competing beliefs cause so much conflict – identity is at stake."*

There are two essential steps to providing a solution here and the second of them needs a lot of explanation. So, the steps first:

- Accept the need to believe.
- Decide for yourself how you will believe.

I could easily give this entire chapter and the rest of the book to the iconic 90s *X-Files* series and the steadfastness of Fox Mulder's background in his office where a UFO poster with the inscription "I want to believe" hang for the entire nine seasons of the show and even showed up in both movies that followed it. When Mulder says, "I want to believe so badly in a truth beyond our own," in a seventh season episode called "Closure" he's articulating a deep need felt by all of us.

Sigmund Freud, ahead of his time, cited the need to believe by saying that those who professed themselves to be atheists did so with the same fervour of belief as those who were devout Christians.

The beliefs we hold are the result of a mix of environmental factors, cultural influence, and upbringing. In many ways our beliefs hold us. But we are not passive containers of those beliefs. Our constantly evolving inner state allows us to reappraise our perception of reality strengthening or weakening particular beliefs we hold.

This implies that we have actual, indirect control over our beliefs that is driven by our values. Philosophers give this a fancy name and call it "indirect doxastic voluntarism". Its basic tenet is that by acquiring and appraising additional data we can decide how to apply our beliefs.

In this context Khalid Sheikh Mohammed may not have had a choice in his belief in God but he did have a choice on how he exercised that belief. Actions are led by beliefs. We have already seen in this chapter that expectations and perception play a pivotal role in defining our reality. Values are the foundation of everything because they also determine what is of sufficient value to us to motivate us to invest energy that will lead to action. In that way values both precede and follow beliefs in a complex, mental calculus that leads to action.

Social psychologists who research the connection between values and behavior explain that a belief that sees a particular behavior as a representation of a value is the key requirement for the existence of the relationship between that value and that behavior.

Values then are the key to moderating behavior that appears to be given the green light by our beliefs. So those who, for example, might be inclined to take the Old Testament literally and cite Leviticus 24:17: "Whoever takes a human life shall surely be put to death." may moderate that belief by valuing all human life and considering the flawed nature of human judgement.

We could use Khalid Sheikh Mohammed to explore this further, but he is an admittedly poor example not because his behavior cannot be explained by what I've just said, quite the opposite in fact, but because his actions that led to 9/11 elicit a highly emotive response that clouds our judgement. Add to this the fact that his ethnicity, as well as his religion, are not western and the appraisal mix becomes even more clouded by emotion.

To better clarify how values affect beliefs and beliefs take values into account and lead to specific behaviors we will need to elicit the help of what has often been called America's most hated family.

Values Drive Everything You Do

Viewers who watched documentary maker Louis Theroux's Surviving America's Most Hated Family will be familiar with the Phelps. The subject of a trilogy by Theroux, over a twelve year period, the Phelps family are more familiar to American audiences for their picketing of soldiers' funerals. Acting as members of the Westboro Baptist Church, which numbers 71 and is mostly made up of the Phelps extended family, they'd turn up with homemade signs describing the death of U.S. soldiers in foreign battlefields as "God's revenge on the U.S. for tolerating homosexuality."

As hateful behaviors goes this is neither here nor there these days. The Westboro Baptist Church led, until recently, by the late Fred Phelps, has been remarkably consistent in its anti-gay behavior since 1989, when it sought a crackdown on homosexual activity at Gage Park near its headquarters in Topeka, Kansas.

The reason they make such excellent subjects for my example however lies in their normality. The Phelps women are all-American, pretty by modern standards, with great hair and perfect teeth. The Phelps family members hold regular jobs and are socially decent to those they interact with. They are intelligent, high-achieving and socially adept. They are easy to talk to. They work happily alongside gay people. If a gay person entered their church they'd welcome them in.

Their dysfunction then is in this one activity: their pickets. Louis Theroux has become the expert on them. In a BBC interview he summed up the question on everyone's minds by saying: "What we're trying to do in the documentary is look at an activity that is so antisocial, so strange, so futile and at its worst, so cruel, and we're saying "Why? Why do that?", especially when you seem to be, for the most part, kind and sensitive people."

The answer lies in values, especially the values that make up their core identity. Fred Phelps was, apparently, an angry person who twisted the teachings of the Bible to justify his anger and instilled that anger in his children who passed it to their children. It is easy here to be both judgmental and perplexed. "Why not reject this? Why not go away?" apparently four of Fred Phelps' 13 children did just that. But the Church operates like a closed club. If you leave the family, you're out and on your own. No family member will have any contact with you. Within the Church people form friendships, support each other and are fully engaged in a coherent support network that surrounds you with total acceptance and approval.

Grow up within that environment or buy into its message and it becomes really difficult to leave it without wrenching part of yourself. The price for a feeling of safety and acceptance and help and support whenever you need it is the unquestioning acceptance of Fred Phelps' anger and its target: homosexuality.

The family members who picket U.S. soldiers' funerals and cause so much extra grief to their families and relatives have little choice themselves. The moment they fail to use their own values to regulate their beliefs they are as captive to the inevitable toxicity of those beliefs as Khalid Sheikh Mohammed is in his.

That doesn't excuse either the Phelps or Khalid Sheikh Mohammed. We understand them better, perhaps, but at the same time we can see that they choose the easier path. Belief is not expressed in isolation. It has to be expressed in terms of values, goals, direction in life, identity and purpose.

The Phelps family members who stay in the Westboro Baptist Church and engage in picketing have chosen to accept the beliefs handed down to them without critically examining them or questioning where they take them. What's more they appear adept at mentally compartmentalizing their picketing. Khalid Sheikh Mohammed displayed similar behavior when he took part in the plot that culminated in the attack on the World Trade Center.

Both these examples are admittedly extreme so let's add a smaller, third, by way of a hypothetical experiment: Suppose somebody gave you $1,000 to sincerely believe that pigs can fly?

You cannot honestly believe that pigs are capable of flight because every credible piece of evidence we have of how the world works suggests the opposite.

Even though it would benefit you materially to try and believe what your potential benefactor is asking of you, you can't because one of the values we all hold dear is truth. We hold that dear because it leads to a clear understanding of reality. We need to feel we understand reality to function safely and plan in order to survive. Self-preservation and prediction are the brain's sole prime directive and prime function, respectively. Our beliefs then are filters based on our values that determine our attitude. Attitude leads us to behavior. This is the chain that leads from the internal states of our being to the external, observable actions we take.

Being intentional in our beliefs requires us to dig deep into our core values and understand who we are and where we want to go in the course of our lifetime.

Core values are critical to how we think and behave. As a result, they contribute to our resilience, which is why we are going to examine them next.

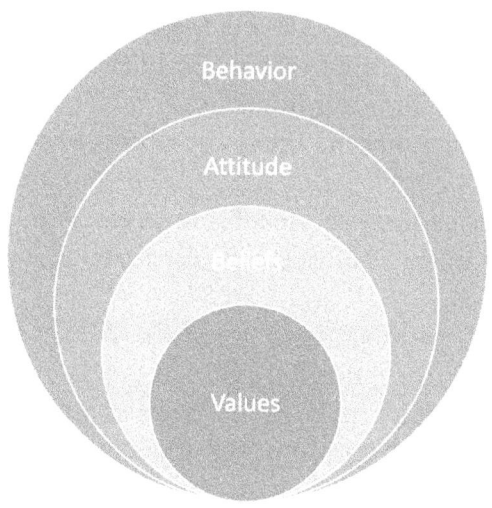

Fig. 6-4. External behavior is driven by internal beliefs that are regulated by core values.

Points to Remember

- Beliefs are the backseat drivers of our behavior.
- Intentionality is goal-orientated behavior in which an individual uses strategies to achieve various ends or effects.
- Relationships are, for the most part, inherently difficult to get right.
- Without commonly accepted boundaries communication is difficult.
- Values are key to moderating behavior that is driven by our belief system.
- The need to believe is strong in all of us.
- How we believe is a personal choice.
- A brain prepared to deal with the unexpected deals with the unexpected better than a brain that hasn't.
- We have evolved to see patterns everywhere and ascribe meaning to everything.
- Our beliefs and our sense of identity are tightly intertwined.

Question Time

- What beliefs do you hold that drive your behavior?
- How do your values moderate your beliefs?
- Are you aware of the process?

Top Tip

- Define for yourself a core belief that, like an ideal, you can use to guide yourself through life.

7. Values

From a conceptual perspective history is easy to read. The 19th century was all about industrialization. We harnessed machines to augment manual labor by many degrees of magnitude. The 20th century was about achieving efficiencies of scale so the machines that create our goods could run better and produce more at lower cost. The 21st century is about resilience as the production hubs and supply networks we have created are stress-tested to the limit.

The global pandemic that started in the closing months of 2019 acted as a catalyst that accelerated change everywhere. The additional environmental and psychological pressure it piled up became a scalpel that exposed all our weaknesses. The one attribute that would perhaps have allowed us all to weather the Covid-19 storm better, that would have allowed our systems of governance and systems of trade to weather it better: resilience, appeared to be missing from our arsenal. Interestingly, this is where values come in.

There is a chain of causal attributes we need to work our way through now. For example, we can't talk about values without tackling personality and we can't tackle personality without discussing traits. Traits, in turn, affect goals, motivation and behavior. We need to spell out the difference between personality and character, two qualities that are often used interchangeably, and we also must define the difference between traits and values which are also two qualities that are also misunderstood and are often used interchangeably.

When all the tools we had at our disposal to help us do all this were solely in the province of philosophy and psychology we could afford to fudge the area between all these qualities because we believed that theories on each one were tinged with personal preferences and opinion. Today however we have powerful fMRI machines that allow us to see the thinking brain as it thinks and determine just what is structural and ingrained and what is acquired and learned. We can see the neural signatures generated when particular traits kick in or specific values are taken into account.

This leads us to better understand what can be mitigated and regulated and what can be directed and controlled.

Traits, we understand, are largely ingrained. Values are largely cognitive. Traits however directly impact values and values, in turn, indirectly affect traits. For example, someone who is musically gifted, a trait that is based on specific physical and neural attributes, will consider playing music and learning to play a musical instrument as a form of self-expression and creativity, a value. The exercise of that value will strengthen their musical gift.

It is in this link between traits and links and the strength of the associative bond that develops between them that we best see the exercise of intentionality that allows us to consciously and actively direct who we become.

Traits vs Values

If I placed a sword in your hands and asked you to behead a person held powerless in front of you, would you do it? If you answer "No" you will explain your denial by citing the universally held value of the sanctity of life. To universally understand your position here we must codify it. Social psychologist Shalom Schwartz created a motivational continuum that explains the many different behaviors humans exhibit. In that continuum the refusal to behead another person on the basis of the value placed on human life is filed under 'Benevolence'.

If I next also placed a pistol to your head and ordered you to do it, would you do it then? Self-preservation is one of the few instincts we have, and 'Security' is also a universal Schwartz value. Now, you might find yourself caught between two warring values inside you. On the one hand you know that killing another human being, especially a helpless one is wrong. On the other hand, like every other human on the planet, you're programmed to act to survive.

You may think that, in the scenario I have just painted, you have no choice. In order to survive you will have to transgress against one of your dearest values and kill another, helpless, human being. So, let me now add one more variable to this. I may be holding a gun to your head but you are stronger than me by several orders of magnitude. Would you now kill someone else to survive?

Physical strength is a trait. As such it directly impacts upon the values we have and changes how we apply them. You may, for instance, hold the belief that the strong must protect the weak. That means you believe that strength must be used to right the imbalance of the world. Your superior strength then, places upon you the responsibility to act where many others wouldn't.

This is what I usually call "The Spiderman Dilemma." To paraphrase the refrain of our friendly, neighborhood Spiderman, the moment you have a choice where others wouldn't you are faced with the obligation to exercise it. But that obligation only arises when you have values, not traits. Someone, just as strong, who values only survival is more likely to choose to execute a helpless human being rather than act in a way that will jeopardise their own safety.

Indeed, in the Spiderman origin tale, the superhero's civilian alter-ego, Peter Parker does not actively choose to do the right thing until his omission to do so in the first instance results in a personal tragedy that teaches him a valuable lesson.

Spider Man's dictum, "With great power comes great responsibility" alternatively known as the Peter Parker principle is in accord with superhero behavior that harnesses special abilities into a specific moral code. Captain America's catchphrase "I can do this all day", Batman's unspoken code of not killing his adversaries though he, himself, can be killed are overt expressions of sacrifice and great personal risk.

Prior to the superhero culture societies found other ways to encode and communicate the values they thought led to behavior that benefited the majority. In ancient Greek mythology Hercules' twelve labors were a journey of redemption transforming a powerful demi-god into a moral being. Outside western culture, the exploits of the Sumerian mythical hero Gilgamesh, provide the guidance needed for ethical behavior.

Even in *The Lord of The Rings*, Gandalf makes a point about not killing those who seemingly deserve it because one cannot, equally, give life to those who have been unfairly killed. That same point in a different context and therefore different perspective is later echoed by Wonder Woman's admonition over caring for the weak. "…it's not about what you deserve, but about what you believe." She says to the god of war, Ares in refusal to stop protecting humans.

What we learn from these examples is that culture always finds a way to encode the guidance it needs to instruct the individual on the best behavioral standards possible. While, from a distance, this may seem like some grand plan orchestrated by some mysterious, invisible architect it is nothing more than natural evolution. The societal constructs we create require rules that help us navigate them otherwise the chaos that will ensue from our unruly behavior will cause them to collapse.

Superheroes are the latest representation of the cultural artifacts used to enshrine those rules and present them in a way that makes it easy for them to be widely consumed by individuals and shared amongst communities.

This way, well-intentioned messages about standing up for peers and protecting others, exhibiting courage, practising self-sacrifice and self-control, and cultivating willpower become part of our own understanding of how the world expects us to function so we can be a part of it.

The reason so much time, effort, creativity and energy goes into all this is because intuitively we know that values are the only means through which we learn to regulate our individual traits. In a ground-breaking study Bremen university social psychology researchers recruited 1,867 participants to posit their social construct theory. They summarized their findings with: "Personal values are reliable cross-situational predictors of attitudes and behavior."

Social constructionism is the theory that our perception of reality is based upon shared assumptions. Its proponents believe that much of what we learn about the world is derived from a social context. There is much to be unpacked in this statement and a lot to consider but we need to first backtrack just a little. Social constructionism was based on even more ground-breaking work and original insights on basic human values made by the social psychologist Shalom Schwartz.

Schwartz started from the basic proposition that values are cognitive representations of universal evolutionary-based motives that are rooted in the very real, everyday biological needs of individuals. By looking at this alongside the need of the individual for coordinated social interaction, and the directly derived need for survival and well-being of the social groups that are formed when individuals get together, Schwartz was able to arrive at a set of universal values. His research, cultural studies, and social experiments across 20 countries generated confidence in the identification of a set of values that can be called "basic" and "universal".

Something that is the building block of other things, much like the atom of classical physics is of the matter we see around us, is usually perceived to be discrete and sequential. Yet study atoms deeply enough and you begin to understand that the subatomic world is made up of a continuum of probabilities where, in certain contexts, some of which are more likely than others.

The values identified by Schwartz and his associates are similar to sub-atomic physics in that respect. Schwartz suggested that rather than view them as discrete qualities, they represent a continuum made up of five, roughly, opposing pairs arranged in a flywheel arrangement. Where the needle points at in each pair's part of the outer edge of that flywheel depends, very much, upon context, beliefs and goals. This, integrative approach to personality shows two distinct things first, how we can each be unique despite sharing the exact shame values and second, the degree to which we can self-direct our responses and control our behavior even when the traits we have pre-dispose us to act in a particular way and hold some specific beliefs.

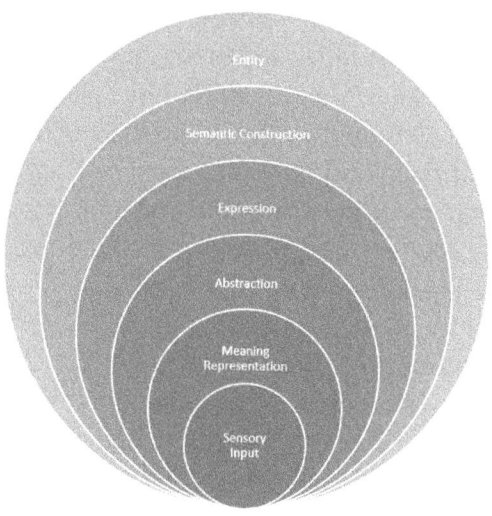

Fig. 7-1. The abstractions that give rise to our complex sense of agency and being have physical foundations in the way we capture and then process sensory information.

Being intentional, in this context, is not just a case of willing our self to hold specific values. That is an easy thing to do and in most cases only leads to increased internal anxiety as the gap between our professed values and our actions widens and we experience an ever increasing degree of cognitive dissonance.

Being intentional requires the closing of the gap between what we say or acknowledge what we value and what we do. Our actions really do speak louder than our words. Our choices can betray our true beliefs and reveal our real feelings.

The path to becoming who we really want to become starts with better understanding who we are.

Character vs Personality

Who you are, right now, is the sum total of everything that's happened to you and the way you handled it. Who you become depends on your choices and decisions. What you choose is based on what you value. What you value is linked to where your life is going. Without a direction we have no purpose. Without purpose our values disappear because we have no reason to hang onto any of them. We then become slaves to the circumstances that create each moment of our life.

In biology, there is a clear-cut definition between character and personality. Field researchers regard character as "any observable feature, or trait, of an organism, whether acquired or inherited. An acquired character is a response to the environment; an inherited character is produced by genes transmitted from parent to offspring."

When to comes to humans however the definition lands us straight into hot water. Are we the sum of our nature or our nurture? Is everything about us pre-determined because of our genes and place of origin or do we have the means to mitigate the former and regulate the latter so we can become who we want to become?

The argument is, basically, the classic debate of nature vs nurture with a few additional twists thrown in. It is easy, at this point to wash our hands off all responsibility for who we are. We can say that we are either unable or incapable of overcoming our biological destiny. It is impossible to avoid our environmental fate.

Or, we could go the other way and lay blame for our inability to do so at our very own footsteps. We can easily call our self 'weak', 'fragile', 'insecure', lacking motivation and self-awareness. Incapable of rising from where we initially found ourselves left by circumstances. In this approach we usually find able and willing allies in the popular media that is quick to talk about "self-made" success stories and highlight individuals who rose above their initial conditions despite the odds they faced. And popular culture where the myth of the stand-alone success story persists because it feeds into our need to believe we can make it without help, that we can change, succeed, rise and become better without being beholden to anyone.

Did a cave person version of us whose brain and body had evolved to survive am inherently hostile environment harbor the same degree of self-recrimination and doubt inside them? Idealists, here, will be tempted to say "no" and buttress their case with the argument of simpler times and a more linear world. That is only true in retrospect. The world we live in is always the world we have evolved to live in. It is complex and dangerous, amazing, and wonderful. We are complicated in our behavior, ambivalent in our choices and ambiguous in our values because we have evolved to deal with fluid environments and ever-changing circumstances.

Each moment we examine, whether past or present, is made up of the same elements: a person representing the peak of evolutionary complexity and a world that is constantly challenging. Each of these entities represents a complex, dynamic system that is always striving for balance and is always responding to elements that threaten that balance. Our ability to use what evolution has given us expands in direct response to the scope and magnitude of the challenges presented by the world we live in.

If we are, at times, indecisive, conflicted, torn. If our beliefs, ideas, actions, values, traits, personality and character do not align neatly to aid us, it's because the complexity of the world and the complicated nature of who we are make it naturally hard to achieve such alignment.

I cannot stress this sufficiently. We fail to thrive because we lack the energy we need to succeed. We lack the energy we need because we try to go-it-alone. It takes a village or a community to raise each of us to admirable behavioral heights. Any of us can fall at any time.

To break this down further so that it stops being the platitude it seems consider that nothing can rise from nothing. This means that everything must have a cause, a reason, an origin. A little green ball that moves at speed across a tennis court has been struck by a tennis racquet. The kinetic force that provides the impetus of the tennis ball's movement is invisible to us, but we don't question its existence because we have seen the tennis racquet strike it.

We believe in the kinetic energy that moves the tennis ball without having to learn the three fundamental laws of motion of Newtonian physics, teach ourselves the mathematics of angular momentum or learn about the conservation of energy and the first law of thermodynamics.

The core concept of being intentional is that we behave the way we want to, to achieve what is important to us. But behavior is just like a tennis ball in motion. It is the visible aspect of many invisible forces that act upon it so it can occur. Just like we require a tennis player to hold a tennis racquet and move it so that it can hit a tennis ball for the tennis ball to fly, on its own, across a tennis court, so does personality that exhibits traits we admire require a suitably engineered environment to manifest.

We know this because of zebra finches. More precisely, the handful of generations of zebra finches raised and studied by Bioscience researchers at the University of Exeter, United Kingdom and the University of Hamburg, Germany.

The researchers "measured personality by placing the zebra finches in a new environment and counting the number of features they visited. Some were shy, staying mainly in one place while others explored widely demonstrating a more outgoing personality. Male and female birds were then paired up and allowed to breed. Each clutch of eggs was fostered by another pair just prior to hatching. Offspring personality was measured once they were adults. Offspring size was also measured and was found to be primarily genetically inherited and not significantly influenced by foster parent size."

In what is probably a welcome message to parents of adopted children and offspring of dysfunctional families the world over, personality doesn't appear to be inherited. Nevertheless, there is an increasing body of experimental evidence that shows that inherited phenotypes, the set of observable characteristics of an individual resulting from the interaction of their genotype with the environment, do contribute to who we become.

The link between that inherited portion of our identity most likely resides in inherited neurobiological and physiological traits that result in tendencies or predispositions in specific environmental contexts.

Let's run a thought experiment to clarify this. Suppose tomorrow you received an award for being "an exceptional human being". The achievement you are being lauded for is your character and personality. In your acceptance speech to the adulating crowd that will gather to celebrate is likely to include a reference to your parents, maybe mentions of some of your teachers and even the occasional friend. But truthfully, before you even get to the raised dais from which you will deliver your acceptance speech you need to run your internal diagnostics and answer the basic question: "Who made me who I am?"

The answer to that requires running an analysis familiar to every MBA student that looks at Strengths, Weaknesses, Opportunities and Threats (better known by its acronym: SWOT). In a person though, this requires honest answers to Values: the filters you apply to guide your behavior, Interests: the things you are passionate about which keep you actively engaged with the world, Temperament: your character traits that trigger specific responses. Activities: physical things you engage in that help you feel alive and your Life Mission: the one-sentence summary that defines your purpose in this world.

These form an acronym that's easy to remember: VITAL. It does not however imply that any of this is easy to define. Nor that once you define them, they are forever fixed and 'solved' in your mind.

We are a nested and therefore complex biological system engaged in constant interaction with our environment. We can become distracted and confused, our attention can wane or be depleted. We can easily lose sight of who we are, what we stand for and what we want to do with our life.

The purpose of using this analysis is to create a constant reminder for us to focus on when we feel that we are in danger of losing our way. The process we engage in to sort out the biologically inherited traits we possess from the values and ideas we acquire and which we choose to apply is part of our becoming intentional in our life. This is something we cannot really do if we do not also consider context.

Context and Meaning

Anyone who has run a Google search on their phone instinctively understands the ability of context to change meaning. A search for "pizza" for instance, carried out on a mobile device at noon, on a street corner is more likely to be a call to satisfy hunger than to discover new pizza recipes or research the history of Italy's national dish.

That same search query carried out at a different time of the day on a desktop device which has also been preceded by some research in Italy's history or search queries on the historical roots of certain dishes will deliver significantly different search results.

The difference between the two instances is what we mean by

context. Context changes the search results for the same search query. And it happens to also affect us in a similar way. When the context changes, we can behave in significantly different ways in response to the exact same or remarkably similar sets of circumstances.

Since the way we spend our days leads to the way we live our life it stands to reason that the cumulative meaning derived from the context of each moment of each day determines the meaning of the life we end up with.

It is perfectly OK, I suppose, to live from moment to moment and day to day, doing anything you can to get by and survive until you no longer can. But this book is about how to go through life with a modicum sense of control and a sense of purpose. Context is examined here through this lens.

There are a thousand examples I can use to illustrate the ability of context to provide meaning to specific sensory signals received by the brain. From all of them I will use one drawn from the military because due to the understandably adversarial environment of combat the margin for error in such situations is infinitesimally small. Mistakes have life-threatening consequences and the brain, in response, tends to provide us with sterling examples of its best behavior.

Imagine yourself then, magically transported, in an active combat environment. Replace the comfort of your everyday life with a situation in which your senses are bombarded by the noise of whizzing bullets passing near your head. Explosions happening all around you. The sound of weapons being fired, and orders being barked.

Faced with such sudden, existential threat your behavior, understandably, will be to duck for cover and make yourself as small a target as possible or, freeze on the spot. Either way the chances of your making it out alive are small. Trained soldiers can function in that environment because their brain have come to understand what is important and what is not. The way their brain does that is by dialling down its attention to specific sensory input and dialling it up to others. Seen through a trained soldier's eyes that, extremely hostile to us, environment is decoded entirely differently.

The bullets whizzing by our head that make us instinctively want to duck and curl up in terror are dismissed as misses that can be ignored, particularly if they consistently fail to get closer to us. Explosions are assessed in terms of calibre and potential threat from fragments. The deafening sound of combat around us that makes it impossible for us to process anything meaningful is mitigated so that directional sounds that allow us to process a threat are given higher priority than say, the firing of a friendly weapon next to us. And voices that may carry vital information or a command are let through so we can actually hear them, much the same way you may hear your name said across the room in a relatively loud and confusing party.

The name given to that, repeatedly proved experiment, is "The Cocktail Effect" and it shows that the brain takes in all the sensory information provided to it by the environment but then filters it through its perception of what is important and what isn't based on its experience and training.

In a cocktail party we know that our name mentioned from across the room is an important signal for us to focus on. In an active combat situation trained soldiers experience the exact same affect applied to battlefield-related signals of noise, sound and movement.

Both the battlefield and the cocktail party provide us with a wall of jumbled noise to process. The brain uses context to filter the signals that are meaningful to us from the noise reported by our senses. The way it does that guides our behavior. At the same time, it reveals our values by the way it apportions the energy required to filter the signals it receives and direct its attention on what we feel is important to us.

Shalom Schwartz's groundbreaking insight was that values are the filter we apply to turn biological impulses we all experience into actionable behavior. By considering context we need to understand how Schwartz's fundamental values are arranged on the flywheel design he imagined, how they affect us and how context changes them and our behavior.

Shalom Schwartz's flywheel of values shows that as a recent analysis of it put it:

> *"values form a circular motivational continuum, meaning that the items do not have exact limits between the values and thus have a shared load on more than one, giving rise to multicollinearity. Additionally, measuring as they do different aspects, each value is multidimensional, thereby reducing internal consistency coefficients."*

We find it hard to be consistent with our self, let alone other people and situations.

From an operational perspective our brain is simple. It has one Prime Directive. To help us survive. To do that it functions like a predictive machine, taking in masses of data from the environment; through our senses and filtering it through its awareness of the situation we are in, our memories of the past and our own personal wealth of knowledge.

You can test this by asking yourself how you know you are safe right now, as you are reading this. Break down each piece of information you have of your environment and understand, for yourself, how you know what it means. Ask yourself where do your assumptions come from? What memories and knowledge do you possess that allows you to determine that your living room or study, right now, are safe for you and you can switch off and divert your attention to this book?

Context is created out of all that. It takes something which you may hear like a car exhaust misfiring and filters it so that your brain derives its meaning and knows it is not threat to you. In a battlezone you would feel your adrenaline rushing and your heartbeat spiking as you sought to determine the exact nature of threat posed by that very same noise.

When something is fundamental it means it is the same for all of us. When Shalom Schwartz came up with the idea of fundamental values common to everyone, he essentially opened the door to the charge that he lumped everyone together even though demonstrably we are all different.

Sharing the same core values with countless other people however doesn't mean we all behave in the exact same way. At the level of the individual our memories are different. Our store of knowledge is different. Each of us has different experiences. We have developed different perspectives to specific things and each of us has different triggers. Our plans are different and our motivation is also different. As a result, our interpretation of the exact same facts will be completely different.

Context ensures that inside each of us there is a fluidity of our sense of purpose and our awareness of who we are that activates and then mixes each fundamental value differently. CMYK are the letters that, in printing, stand for Cyan, Magenda, Yellow and Black. These four colors however are capable of generating over 16,000 color combinations and millions of hues of each color.

Think of context as the color mixer within each person.

The hues it produces are the different responses that arise from the unique mix of the same fundamental ingredients. We can leave the house in the morning to go to work, for instance having given a lecture to our youngest child on the importance of never lying and just an hour later we can be economical with the truth as we explain to our line manager why a pilot project is running behind time and over budget.

We can only affect what we understand. We can only understand what we can analyze. Our own behavior can be opaque to us at times. Knowing how it is formed, what guides it and why it changes from one situation to the next is key to owning it.

Fig. 7–2. Shalom Schwartz's flywheel of values.

Points to Remember

- Values are cognitive. Traits are ingrained.
- When values are activated and used, they reinforce traits.
- The Spiderman Dilemma obliges us to act on behalf of those who can't.
- Every system has rules of operation.
- Culture guides our values, especially when we haven't articulated them to our self.
- Personal values are reliable predictors of both attitudes and behavior.
- We learn about the world through social context.
- The default, universal values we hold are the result of our neurobiology.

- We evolved to live in this world. We can cope with its complexity.
- The environment we create around us either helps us or hinders us.
- The way we spend our days leads to the we live our lives.
- Context changes the value of everything we perceive.
- We can own our behavior, but we need to understand it first.

Question Time

- What are the universal values you perceive and practise?
- Are you aware of the way context changes your behavior and the values you apply?
- How do you plan your day so that it fits in with the plan you have for your life?

Top Tip

- Examine your home and your office. Identify what helps you work and live better and what makes it harder for you. It can be small things such as a door that always sticks, a lock that's hard to use. A light that flickers before it comes on. Fix these things to create less friction and make the effort required to get through each day, way less.

8.   Grit

Life is difficult for everyone. As *Edward Sharpe and the Magnetic Zeros* sing in their lyrics of the song "Life is Hard": *Do not fear, it's safe to say it here/You will not be called a weakling/Nor a fraud/For feeling the pain of the whole wide world...... Yes, life is hard*

This is the kind of truism we intuitively feel and frequently say to each other without really understanding why. I mean, after all, we evolved to live on this world. It is ours. And it should be easier to experience our journey in it. In the wild, plants, animals even bacteria may have to struggle to gain a foothold in their niche but once they do life has relatively few twists and turns for them. Like us they too have adopted for living in their environment. You could argue here that we, as a species, do not truly live in our environment. We live, instead, in an environment that is largely man-made and has therefore been created by us, for us. But then life should be even easier. What we have is more or less, custom-made.

That is true in the sense that survival is no longer a struggle. But that doesn't make life easier. The reason for this apparent anomaly lies in what we are and what the world is. We, as individuals and even as a collective, are a system. We are a complex, nested system which means that our component parts are also complex systems in their own right. The heart, for instance, or the brain are made up of many subsystems which need to work correctly for them to function. The world is also a complex, nested system. The fit between us and the world however is imprecise. The world and our self are two separate, distinct complex systems and each is governed by a different internal logic.

To illustrate this a little better let's take cars and roads as a somewhat crude example. In our man-made environment, and even out in nature, we create roads to take us where we want to go in the shortest possible time and for the least possible effort. But following this systemic logic roads expand and grow and stretch and criss-cross and interconnect until we can no longer get to where we want quickly and efficiently on our own.

So, we build cars that can travel these roads at speed and take us to our destination much easier and faster. The cars make the possibility of longer roads feasible. We then build longer roads, but then we need cars with the capacity of ever greater speeds to get us further, faster. This intertwined complexity has a cost. The World Health Organization estimates that 1.35 million of us die in car accidents every year and between twenty and fifty million suffer an injury, with many incurring a disability. The roads and the cars we create are not intended to kill us. The cars we drive were not created to specifically pollute the environment and damage our health nor were they made to intentionally affect the climate of the planet which makes economic conditions ever more difficult.

Roads and cars have their own system logic. We use them because of our specific systemic needs. But though they were made to serve us, the need for sustainable efficiency in each step along the way, means that we apply solutions that will create problems that will need to be solved the moment they can no longer be ignored.

The internal logic of each system makes it run at its own speed and service its own needs. Most times, like when we speed to get to a meeting on time, our intent and the system's fit in well enough to get the job done that one time. But the fit is always inexact. The world always grates against us because of that, and we always have to work to make sure we fit in it "well enough" to survive and thrive.

This is why need grit. So, what is grit, exactly?

The American Psychological Association defines grit as "a personality trait characterized by perseverance and passion for achieving long-term goals." It sounds a little like goals and motivation which we have already explored or attitude which we shall explore next. In truth grit is all of these things. It is an integral aspect of resilience which we explored in detail in chapter 5. We could then overlook grit completely, gloss over some of its aspects and integrate it into the overall positive life outlook attitude and mindset approach. That's an approach that was often taken in the past, even by experienced psychology researchers, and that's exactly the issue.

New research shows that grit is a defining trait that can alter outcomes for us, provided we are aware of it, how it works, the way it affects us and how we can cultivate it.

In looking at grit, here, as a trait that can alter individual outcomes, we seek to answer three distinct questions:

- Is grit a trait we somehow just have, or can it be acquired?
- Is grit all we need for success in business and life or are there additional caveats?
- How is grit different from resilience and can one exist without the other?

Six studies whose participants ranged from school children to West Point cadets seemed to answer all three questions with a resounding "yes" to grit as a trait that can make a real difference, can be acquired and exists independent of resilience. Positive psychology researcher Angela Duckworth came to popular prominence thanks to a TED Talk about grit that went viral. Clear, concise and backed by data; her talk seemed to say "grit is all we need" if we are to succeed. Her paper on the subject published a year after her talk cites grit as the sole, best indicator for "retention in the military, the workplace, school and marriage,".

In this regard grit is sexy because it can be measured quickly, acquired via a structured approach and it can be improved. I'd love to be able to say that here, now, in my next few words I will give you a sure-fire formula that will allow you to super-charge your grit quotient, measure how it grows and laser-target it to specific tasks so you never, ever, fail at anything again. Unfortunately, I can't.

When I was researching and writing *The Sniper Mind*, over 300 interview hours with elite soldiers, showed me directly just how hard it is to be able to double down and focus on something specific and see it through when your every thought and emotion is urging you to drop it and just give up. Navy SEALs going through the toughest part of their BUD/S training known as "Hell Week", baseball players looking down the narrow funnel that links them to a pitcher with the attention of tens of thousands of fans focused on them and the fate of the game riding on their shoulders, basketball players taking the key shot with the clock running down, students from a low-income, single-parent family concentrating on academic excellence, these are all examples of grit.

They all have something in common. A process, if you like, that starts with something and then feeds into something else. It is a cascading chain of emotional connections that holds firm against negative emotions like doubt and fear and very real negative sensations like pain, hunger, extreme fatigue, and exhaustion. The catalytic point of this chain is indeed grit, the ability to clench your teeth and hold on, but what makes it possible to do so well beyond the point of teeth clenching is what grit leads to and activates.

Just like an anchor, on its own, is powerless to stop a ship from drifting with the current, Grit alone, is insufficient to help us control our lives. It may make us stubborn. We may commendably refuse to give up. Captain America, again, getting up time and again after he's been knocked down in a fight against a physically superior opponent and declaring "I can do this all day," is stubbornness. It is tenacity. It is, yes, grit. But what makes the Captain formidable is that beyond the figurative anchor point provided by grit, he also possesses all the other links of the chain.

He knows who he is. He knows his "why" and his "where". Determining "how" now becomes a little easier. So, the chain of cascading emotional connections that holds us together when the going gets tough looks like this: Grit>Narratives>Identity>Purpose>Life.

The Safe Anchor System Of The Self

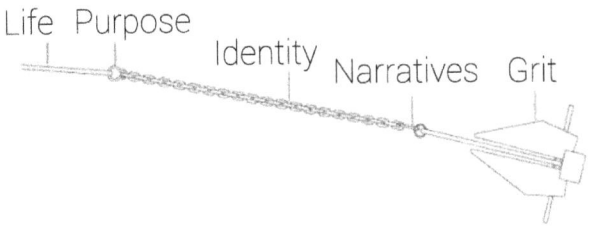

Fig. 8-1. The Safe anchor system of the self against the currents that may set us adrift in life.

Captain America, as a superhero created to specifically become a moral compass, manages to project unshakable faith in himself and what he stands for and what he does, no matter what. So, we may think he has everything worked out. And we do not. If Steve Rogers could talk to us, really, about who he is and what he does he would most probably express the same degree of uncertainty and doubt we all feel when we contemplate our life choices and direction and what we do as part of it all.

Just like an anchor stops a ship from drifting with the tides grit helps us stay the course, be persistent and tenacious. But it's not enough. A ship's anchor is only as good as its chain. And the emotional and psychological chain of cascading links that forms our chain is made up of narratives, identity, purpose, and the direction of our life.

It is, of course, way more complex than that and each of these elements can be broken down to constituent parts. But by having this general image in our head we understand better just what it is that enables us to display grit and 'anchor' our self in place against all odds.

Actor, Emma Watson shot to instant stardom as Hermione Jean Granger in the *Harry Potter* franchise. She was only nine at the time and, as a result of the films' success had to grow up in the public eye. She summed up her experience in a speech she gave: "Becoming yourself is really hard and confusing, and it's a process,".

Part of that process, the part of it where grit is the key anchoring ingredient is what we need to establish for ourselves.

Where Does Grit Come From?

Every superhero needs a good origin story. Somehow, without one, we fail to understand how he operates and why. Grit, is no different. When we see it exhibited we ask where did it come from? How is it formed? Why do some people have it and others don't?

What we are really asking however is how can we have some too?

To answer that last question we, essentially, need to answer all the ones before it. And to do that we need to deconstruct grit and truly understand what it means beyond the semantic meaning of the word itself.

The Cambridge English Dictionary defines grit as: "courage and determination despite difficulty" and in the popular press it is conflated with the ability to keep on going and just not accept giving up as an option. But grit alone, like courage on its own do not make for a win scenario.

A person can exhibit great courage but end up throwing their life away. We can determinately "stay the course" but lack any real ability, opportunity or talent that could take us where we hope to go towards and all our effort, commendable as it may be, can turn into a total waste. The late Hollywood film director Ed Wood, who was posthumously awarded a Golden Turkey Award for Worst Director of All Time in

1980, certainly made up what he lacked by way of talent with grit, but that didn't make his films and books any better.

Grit may be expressed through tenacity, perseverance and obstinance but its true origin, the small, constituent parts that allow it to be formed so it can appear during those crucial, life-defining moments when we need it, lie elsewhere.

Developmental psychologists tell us that grit is basically conscientiousness by another name and everything sexy we uncover about it now, we've known all along. Over decades, studies have shown that every individual's personality falls somewhere along the mix supplied by the "Big Five" personality traits: Openness, Conscientiousness, Extraversion, Agreeableness and Neuroticism. Conscientiousness is made up of self-control, industriousness, responsibility, and reliability.

In the last two years constant refinements in fMRI technology have enabled the study of the thinking brain. Correlations have emerged as a result that show how specific neural architecture in centers of the brain that control executive function and mental set shifting determine, at least in part, just how conscientious we are capable of being.

Executive function is the name we give to the set of mental skills that include working memory, flexible thinking, and self-control. Mental set shifting is part of the executive function and involves the ability to unconsciously shift attention between one task and another. Task switching allows the brain to adapt to changing situations quickly and efficiently so that mental resources are not wasted.

Avoiding wastage and doing more with less is the brain's super power. It is also its Achilles Heel. The human head is of a particular size. This limits the useful real estate available for neural circuitry to form and take up. As a result each neural center in the brain is recruited to perform more than one role. This makes the brain hard to study because everything in it is interconnected. If you think that people are complicated consider that the central processing unit that powers our cognitive functions and processes our emotions is the ultimate social network.

The strength of ties between its different areas, the strength of the signal felt in response to particular contexts and the sheer density of its connections create an environment where the past is important because of its association, the present is key because of its context and the future is vital because of its expectations. Context, in the brain, is hard to unravel because so much of it is hidden from us.

At the same time, intuitively, we know that what builds us up, what enables us to reach our goals and succeed in our plans, is not the sudden decision or desire to do something or become something, but the incremental but sustained focus on the potential we feel within us; the possibilities we constantly aim towards. This drip-effect of success is no accident.

Neuroscientific studies employing fMRI techniques have mapped specific areas of the brain that are activated when grit and conscientiousness are on display in our active decision making. These neuroanatomical correlates of grit suggest that our earliest years play a role on our subsequent, adult, ability to focus on goals and work consistently to achieve them.

If we consider that grit is an emergent trait that requires the activation and coordination of a number of other personality traits and they, in turn, arise out of the biochemical activation of specific brain structures, it stands to reason that the foundation of those brain structures was laid out in our earliest years by the brain processing the signals reported by its sensorium.

Small things like being punctual, learning to complete small tasks, understanding the expectations of others and working to deliver to those expectations, and the help and encouragement we received as we strove to consistently deliver to expectations become the building blocks for much grander character traits later in adult life.

The Jesuit maxim that goes "Give me the child for the first seven years and I'll give you the man" springs to mind here. Often credited to the founder of the order, Ignatius of Loyola, the saying actually goes back a lot further back in time and is historically attributed to Aristotle which shows, I suppose, that the effort to understand our own origin story, as adults, is a constant throughout history.

Since grit then is, partially at least, the result of brain structures and networked neural centers that originate in our earliest experiences of the world the question we now need to answer is the same one Sarah Connor struggled with in the *Terminator* film franchise: is the future fixed or can it be changed by acting differently in the present?

The Stories We Tell

We are natural-born storytellers. We respond to stories, books, films and songs because our brain can recognize the structure, and code the salient points of each story. This helps us understand the context which means we understand the motivation of those involved. The Trojan War makes little socio-economic sense to us but the idea that love trumps politics and pride trumps logic allows us to understand why ten years later the Greeks were still there fighting and killing and dying. Spiderman's ethics may be logical but without the backstory of his tragic personal loss they make little real sense.

Things need to make sense to us in order for our brain to categorize them successfully and prioritize their importance to us in terms of our own context. Our own needs. Before books and films we told stories and poems. Homer's *Iliad* and the poem *Beowulf* capture our imagination because we can decode their meaning and restructure it inside our heads not in a word-for-word model but in an emotive roller-coaster of affective landmarks.

Without making a conscious effort we remember the basis of the storyline, understand the rollercoaster ride of the protagonists' actions and empathize with the dilemmas they face as they make their decisions.

How is that even possible though? None of us were alive in pre-historic Greece or in 700AD when *Beowulf* was composed. Even more to the point we understand that you can't just gather your buddies and go and destroy someone's land and kill all its people just because one of them eloped with one of yours. We all know that Grendel is a fantastical being and that dragons don't exist. None of this stops us from enjoying the storyline of each and feeling that we learn something from it each time we read it or, more likely these days, watch it. But what is it exactly that we learn each time?

To understand that and also see exactly why past experiences, despite their ability to structure the brain, do not totally determine who we are; we must get a quick primer on how memory works and the key role narrative plays in learning.

There are basically two types of memory: working memory, also known as short term memory, and long term memory. The three pressing items you have to attend to as you sit at your desk and your working day kicks off are your working memory. Think of it as a read/write area with finite capacity. You hold the tasks you have to do for the 'next moment'. Each task you perform is written off this mental list and, because it is not that great at storing everything, if it gets overloaded with stored information it will overwrite something else. This is why an emergency to deal with at work will make you forget to pick up the dry cleaning on your way home.

Long term memory is the place where events, facts and figures from short term memory that you judge have lasting value go to be categorized and stored in. The primary differences here is that unlike short term memory that is primarily sensory in nature and of limited capacity, long term memory is semantic in nature and infinite in capacity.

The emergency you had to deal with at work which made you forget to pick up your life partner's gift for their birthday, for instance, is now an event that is associated with unpleasant memories you want to avoid in future. The association shifts into your long term memory and affects the way you plan your work on the day your life partner has their birthday so as not to repeat the disappointing experience you had.

Because long term memory is semantic it involves a number of neural centers in the brain. It pulls in information from the entire sensory spectrum, and it can be triggered by events that are tangential to the specific information that has been stored.

This is a hugely glossed-over account of how memory works but it provides us with the essential floorplan we need to understand it. It remains for me then to stress two additional things: First, the process of capturing information, the encoding that goes on as the brain stores it, transforms the information itself so that it often bears no resemblance to its original form but retains its meaning. Second, information retrieval, the process through which stored memories are recalled is different for each type of memory. Short term memory recalls things sequentially while long term memory is associative. The ease of memory recall, in turn, is dependent on the strength of the ties between memories and that strength depends on the importance of the memory to us and, it is subject to degradation through time,

The complexities that are labelled actions, reactions, strong motivation, values and beliefs arise out of the brain's one-word imperative: survive. We've seen that in order to do that it has to try and predict what will happen next. In order to do that it has to understand what it is it sees, hears, thinks and feels. Meaning is the means through which the brain creates the movie of the world and places us in its central plot line, as its main character.

This is more than a fancy analogy. By definition narrative takes a sequence of events and creates a meaningful order out of them, that generates sense within its context.

The mind makes sense of the world by running a narrative that's very similar to the movies we watch. What we perceive as major events tell us where we are in the story and why: we are born, we grow up, we become trained in something, we get married, we have children, jobs change, friends die.

These are stitched together by smaller events and bit players. The waiter who brings us coffee at a business meeting in a café may look buff and strong but he's a bit-player in our narrative. A backdrop prop that populates the workings of our world and provides stitching instances we use to unlock its secret code. The waiter stands as a marker for a lower-end, service-industry job that signifies the existence of a part of the economy that works on low-margin commodities (like coffee).

To understand his importance in our narrative consider that when he brings the coffee we ordered and goes away all he's really done is he's ensured that the world we know is functioning in a way we consider the norm, and we need to focus on the importance of our meeting. But should he suddenly disappear from the picture. Should the café have no waiters whatsoever because they are impossible to get and we have to get up from our table and make our own coffee, it would signal a fundamental disruption to the economy. Our understanding of how things work would change and we would need to look closely at the world around us to better comprehend the socioeconomic upheaval that marks the end of waitressing as an option and the further impact such a change would have.

It's by constantly taking in and analyzing such micro-instances which stitch together the more significant events we pay attention to that we can predict what will happen next (and why). This allows us to have a certain sense of trust in the world. This saves us precious mental and psychological resources so we can plot the course of our lives. We create the larger narrative we star in out of micro-instances.

The narratives we create define who we are and activate the brain's default mode network that we now know also contributes to our sense of core values and our ability to display grit when under pressure. This makes micro-instances a critical component of the mentalizing we employ when we build our internal models of reality. More pithily put: every moment counts.

Everything that we now know about the brain's structures and their operation tells us that the narrative our brain constructs is a key part of our understanding of reality. How well that understanding works determines the type of choices we make, the decisions we take and the actions that follow them.

Because narrative has a structure which, just like a movie, has important events that are like peaks and relative mundane lulls, that are like the troughs in a film's plotline, it creates memorable events of greater importance that can be used to enhance both our memory of specific events and our understanding of their importance relative to us.

We only learn because we can remember. We can only remember when what we've learnt has been structured in a narrative. Narrative takes a sequence of events and creates meaningful order that generates sense in time and space (which is why narratives always have a beginning, middle and end) and creates meaning in relation to its surroundings (which is why narratives always have context). This has deeper implications for marketers and content creators and, also, for each of us struggling to curate our own sense of who we are in the time and space of our own life.

Contemporary neuroscience has fancy terminology for all this. It describes the process via which narratives help create our sense of self as "temporal synchrony and the binding problem, the action-perception circuit in cognition, and the mirroring processes of embodied intersubjectivity". For those who haven't encountered it before, in its most general form, "The Binding Problem" concerns how items that are encoded by distinct brain circuits can be combined for perception, decision, and action. To us, all of this, translates as the somewhat more prosaic: Each person's story only makes sense in the context of their time and place.

Paul J. Zak who is credited with coining the term "neuroeconomics" and is the man behind the discovery of the behavioral effects of the neurochemical called oxytocin, also discovered that compelling narratives cause oxytocin release in the brain and have the power to affect our attitudes, beliefs and behaviors.

At this point contemporary neuroscience literally joins hands with the more traditional phenomenological philosophy that dates back to Plato and Aristotle. Both busy themselves to understand the structures of consciousness as experienced from the first-person point of view. The central structure of an experience is its intentionality, its being directed toward something, as it is an experience of or about something objective.

In that regard narratives, stories, help create a deeper sense of shared identity. They generate meaning and foster cooperative actions through neurochemical correlates that kick into motion as the brain responds to the narrative and release elevated levels of oxytocin. Context fixes our sense of who we are in relation to where and when we are.

The way narrative does that has an underlying structure or pattern that is always the same. This is why Joseph Campbell's 1949 book *The Hero With A Thousand Faces* that examines the mythological structure of the journey of the archetypal hero found in world myths, has never fallen out of popularity.

Campbell's study resonates with us because we readily identify the storytelling structure our brain responds to. We understand that really, when it comes to narrative, there is only ever one story with a singular structure and rhythm and pace. We need to become excited. We then become engaged. We then identify with the values and become involved with the characters and storyline.

The process works the same whether it is a story in an ad, the origin tale of a superhero or a brand, the plot of a film, the storyline in a book or what you tell yourself as you go through your day and the collective days take you through your life.

My earliest writings and some of my current professional work revolves around search and search marketing. In the digital world we employ structured data on websites. Structured data is formatted to exist in relational databases that are connected to each other. The reason we employ structured data is because it transforms the unstructured data of content usually found in websites into a format that acquires value and meaning to a machine such as a search engine crawler.

So, structured data helps machines understand the context and meaning of content. Narrative does the same for the brain. It takes a jumble of events, facts, figures and characters and arranges them in a chronological and topological order that helps us make sense of it all and, tellingly, determine its importance in relation to us.

Narrative then, to summarise, is how we index the world. In doing so we also discover our own self. Establishing a chronologically logical sequence to events that generates a cause-and-effect, first-this-then-that structure to everything is important. We need self-knowledge to create the core identity that is responsible for generating values, creating grit and manufacturing the motivation we need to get anything done. But self-knowledge cannot happen without first possessing self-awareness.

Aristotle, somewhat ambitiously said: "Knowing yourself is the beginning of all wisdom." And yet, wisdom is what we use to qualitatively describe the value of judgement made via the synthesis of knowledge, experience and context.

Feelings, Emotions and Actions

In the opening scenes of Bruce Lee's seminal breakthrough film *Enter The Dragon* we are treated to what appears a throwaway scene of Bruce Lee training a young pupil whom he asks to kick him. In that scene Lee gives what is now seen as an important lecture about "emotional content" in unarmed combat and the priority given to feeling over thinking.

Lee insisted in including a lot of his Eastern philosophy in the film and persuaded the director to agree to it. You can find the clip-on YouTube by typing "Bruce Lee on "emotional content"" on the site (or type it in Google).

Lee was ahead of his time in translating the mindset of unarmed combat into everyday layman's terms. The point he makes in the film, is that how we feel determines how we act. Understanding the role emotions play in cognition is key to understanding who we are.

The popular notion that "Emotions cloud the brain" prevents us from facing and understanding a counterintuitive truth that asks us to fully embrace how we feel in order to think, judge and act better.

Intuitively we subscribe to this idea that emotions are something we should suppress because we all have direct, personal experience of some time in our life when we "saw red" and lashed out verbally or physically. We all then, mostly, agree with the notion that being able to appraise facts without getting emotional and remaining in a sort of Vulcan-like state when dealing with complex situations is desirable.

The reason we covet such emotionless state is because we believe that if emotions cloud the brain, an emotionless brain would be driven by logic. It would see facts clearly. It would then fairly and dispassionately choose the available course that is best for us. Our judgement would be better and the outcomes we would get would be more favorable to us.

Except of course, neuroscience has given us a tangible example of the exact opposite, in the case of 'Elliot' who used logic to make decisions and ended up ruining his life. 'Elliot' is a pseudonym used to preserve doctor-patient confidentiality and the anonymity of the patient whose account is included in neuroscientist Antonio Damasio's book *Descarte's Error*.

In it, Damasio talks about how by adopting what he calls "high-reason view" we adopt a purely computational mode that sees us as machines in a purely mechanistic universe where outcomes are determined by the sheer calculation of probable odds. As he puts it this "important aspect of the rationalist conception is that to obtain the best results, emotions must be kept out. Rational processing must be unencumbered by passion."

Except, of course, that "Elliot", a high-functioning, successful business person who worked in the upper levels of a company, happily married and a role model to his younger siblings and colleagues, suffered a brain tumor whose removal damaged the frontal lobe tissue in his brain.

By the time he entered Damasio's care Elliot was a basket case having lost his job, his house and his wife and living on a couch at his younger brother's house. Yet, as one battery of tests after another were to prove Elliot's cognitive faculties were as sharp as ever. His IQ tests were high. His long-term memory, short-term memory, language skills, perception, and handiness with math were all functioning properly. He had all the equipment necessary to make good decisions and, when asked to ideate about possible solutions to a problem he was exemplary.

Yet, Elliot's life was a ruin because he couldn't make plans for the future. Whether that future was a few hours away or days or weeks or months didn't matter. Elliot just could not plan for it.

Damasio's work with Elliot uncovered that the problem lay not in his hard skills and cognitive abilities but in his emotional intelligence. The damage to his frontal lobe had left him unable to process emotion. As a result he was equally detached about everything. Damasio writes in his book: "I began to think that the cold-bloodedness of Elliot's reasoning prevented him from assigning different values to different options and made his decision-making landscape hopelessly flat."

Just like with values, emotions give us direction. When that direction is lacking, when we don't know where we should go then all roads are, indeed, the same and will equally take us there.

What we now know of cognition and motivation shows that without emotional content we find it hard to recognize context, apportion value, prioritize, focus and allocate the necessary resources to see a task to the end. Without emotions goal-orientation becomes hard. Goal-completion becomes virtually impossible as logic dictates that we deal with the present that is pressing us now while the future is distant and uncertain and indistinct and can be put off. Yet it is the future that materializes out of our present actions. And actions in the present that fail to take this into account, in turn, fail to make it materialize.

The final link between grit, emotions, identity, and purpose lies in self-awareness. Elliot, for instance, would have no problem doing the same thing again and again, applying pure logic to unemotionally solve all problems he faced, even though he didn't get the outcome he expected each time. Self-awareness, by definition, is the conscious knowledge of a person's character and feelings.

A Kent State University study that tracked over 200 students showed that grit, the exact same trait that's promoted by Angela Duckworth, does equate to greater academic success but only "through a sequential pathway of mediators including self-efficacy and achievement orientation goals."

Self-efficacy is, virtually, self-awareness with a hefty dose of self-belief.

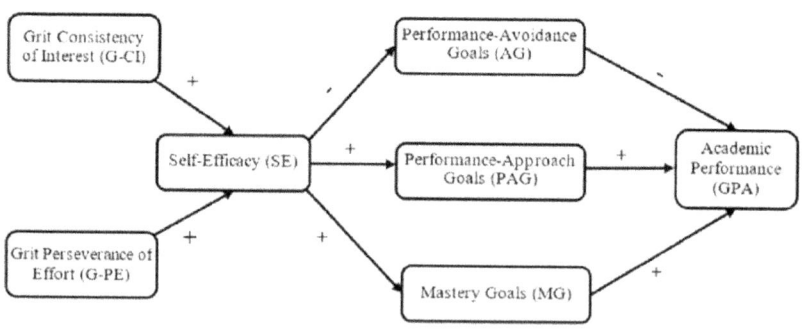

Fig 8-2 Grit Consistency and Grit Perseverance do not lead to positive outcomes without the mediation of self-awareness.

Points to Remember
- Each of us is a complex *nested* system.
- We experience friction in our daily life because we fit imperfectly in the world.
- Grit is the ability to ignore the friction we experience, long enough to get done what we want to accomplish.
- We learn *only* because we can remember.
- Narrative helps us make sense of the things we observe.
- Memory requires narrative.
- Our story makes sense *only* to us.
- Context remind us of who we are because it helps us make sense of where and when we are.
- We index the information of the world through narrative.
- How we feel determines how we act.
- Emotions drive us the same way our values do.
- Our awareness of emotional content allows us to recognize context and assess it.

Question Time
- What is your story? Are you aware of it?
- Are you comfortable acknowledging and embracing your feelings?
- How do you make decisions? Which part of your inner calculus takes into account how you feel and which part uses logic?

Top Tip
- Set yourself a small target for a month that will stretch your ability to stay focused and committed. It can be anything from personal fitness and weight loss to a work related goal. Work out for yourself what you need to do each day to get to your goal by the end of the month.

9.   Attitude

"Lose the attitude" is the one admonition that unites educators and pupils around the globe and across the ages. Beyond the fact about what this says on young pupils' behavior as they seek to establish who they are and how they should behave in the world at an impressionable time of their development, it is of direct interest to us because of what it implies: attitude determines behavior.

Beleaguered teachers have intuitively known this for a long time. So have drill Sergeant Majors. Because the military deals with stark issues of life and death and the margin of error on the battlefield is zero, it has always understood the value of attitude and its power to change behavior.

Attitude, as a word and what it stands for has been part of our vocabulary for such a long time that studies have offered either a vague operational definition of it or none at all. As a result, until the end of the 20th century, whenever social psychologists examined it little effort was made to measure it.

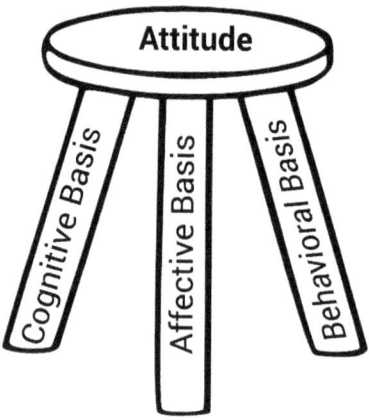

Fig 9.1 Attitude is a fragile construct made up of three distinct elements.

If attitude affects behavior it stands to reason that changing it also changes the way we behave. Since behavior itself arises out of a sequential chain of attributes made up of Expectations, Perception, Reality and Beliefs, it also stands to reason that the attributes that make up attitude are, in turn affected, by it reach across the entire spectrum of our inner world.

Indeed, pioneering studies on subjects gearing up to take life-defining exams and the exemplary work the military has done to create battle-effective soldiers who are capable of not getting killed in an environment that is designed to kill them, show that attitude is made up of a triumvirate of attributes drawn from our behavioral, affective and cognitive life.

The elements that support and form our attitude make for an uneasy balance. Cognition, Emotional Awareness and Behavior create a fragile, nuanced feedback loop where each regulates the others. Attitude is fragile for that reason. At the same time, the right attitude, properly formed and perfectly balanced becomes the platform to reach higher, achieve more and be more than you ever thought is possible.

The military has always used its vast experiential store of knowledge of human behavior in a combat environment, to devise ways to help its soldiers operate with greater focus, self-awareness and fearlessness. To do so it has done what every other tribe does: it has used language both for utility and identity. It chooses words to communicate that articulate a specific reality while, at the same time, create an identity that embraces specific values which are externalized in specific behaviors.

There are countless examples of this. When, for instance, Kevin Lanz, a SEAL team THREE sniper who wrote *The Last Punisher* gives a detailed account of his tour in Ramadi and the bruising battle for the soul of that city he frequently refers to himself in his writing as BTF, shorthand for Big Tough Frogman.

To us, at first glance, it sounds like boasting. It's not. Navy SEALs use the lingo to push themselves through inhumanely difficult conditions that take a heavy toll on the mind and psyche and still maintain operational efficiency. "BTF" in this context is a personal mantra that shields the brain from psychological damage and maintains the cohesion of identity when fear, fatigue and a sense of hopelessness could easily undo it.

Similarly, when U.S. Marines form a seamless brotherhood through the code of honor that's represented by "Semper Fi" a shortening of the Latin Semper Fidelis that means "keep the faith" they too are using language to mean something specific to them which helps them identity who they are.

Marines appear cocky and gang-ho, behavior that is the result of the attitude that goes with their more esoteric motto of: "Embrace the suck". Being called upon to undertake some of the most risky, difficult missions in the world, often against the odds, requires a very specific type of attitude to make you overcome natural emotions such as fear and regulate natural behavior such as risk aversion.

Attitude then is the lubricant that makes the imperfect fit of the complex system that is the individual work more smoothly with the complex system that is the world. Since each of us is a system that needs to somehow fit into the greater system that is the world around us, attitude reduces some of the friction that's created by our imperfect fit. It enables us to get further for less effort.

Prussian General Carl von Clausewitz first experienced war at the age of 12 as an ensign in the army of Fredrick the Great. He took part in the Siege of Mainz and the Prussian army's deeper invasion of France during the French Revolution. Despite seeing active combat at such a young age he went on to have a long, distinguished military career that included stints in the Russian army and he fought in the Napoleonic wars of 1806 to 1815. In his strategic treatise titled *On War* he used detailed empirical data and personal observations combined with Hegel's dialectical method to make deep, logically undeniable points about war.

The world, of course, has always been a large system rubbing against the much smaller systems that fit in it. This is why Clausewitz's description of war resonates with system engineers and system theorists: "Everything in war is very simple," Clausewitz wrote, "but the simplest thing is difficult. The difficulties accumulate and end by producing a kind of friction that is inconceivable unless one has experienced war."

Substitute "life" for "war" and you have the perfect observation of entropy working within systems that fit together without having been created to fit into each other.

"We say a man has strength of character, or simply has character, if he sticks to his convictions, whether these derive from his own opinions or someone else's, whether they represent principles, attitudes, sudden insights, or any other mental force." Clausewitz again.

Strength of character is the result of attitude. Psychology defines strength of character as a way of thinking, feeling and behaving that benefits oneself and others. Our sense of identity, who we are, and our sense of purpose, the why of our existence, are key to regulating our thoughts, emotions and actions.

The 20th century French aristocrat, writer and poet known as comte de Saint-Exupéry (count of Saint-Exupéry) famously said that "The meaning of things lies not in the things themselves, but in our attitude towards them." We need meaning to ascribe value to our actions and make sense of our priorities. Our attitude is a manifestation of the meaning of our existence and the impact that we have on the people around us.

There are many things we can do to better direct our actions, validate our beliefs and better fit in our communities of choice. Of all those things, our attitude, the way we interact with the world is the one trait we can develop that could be considered a shortcut to positive outcomes.

As a tangible example of how attitude is manifested in actions that reveal a lot about a person's cognitive, emotional and behavioral make up I bring up a scene from *The Matrix Reloaded* the second film of the trilogy. In that scene, the Oracle calls Neo away from Zion to give him crucial guidance about the path of the future. When Neo arrives at the address the Oracle has given him, he encounters the Oracle's guardian, Seraph, who proceeds to fight him as a way of certifying that Neo is who he says he is. After his unprovoked physical attack and having established Neo's credentials, Seraph says to Neo: "You do not truly know someone until you fight them."

The Matrix trilogy draws heavily from Chinese philosophy and here, beyond the cinematic appeal of a cryptic message delivered after another acrobatically spectacular martial arts sequence, we also get to think about how stressful situations; like fighting, expose our true nature because we cannot allocate the mental resources required to maintain false facades.

False Fronts And Attitude

The false fronts we maintain are not who we truly are. They don't reflect our real identity. They are a response to our perception of who others expect us to be or who we think we are supposed to be in particular contexts and situations.

Because the world is not designed for us to seamlessly fit into it, each of us, each day is engaged in a personal struggle that's mental, emotional and, in various ways, physical. We may not be actively fighting as in combat, but we are nonetheless engaged in a struggle only we feel, that consumes our cognitive and emotional resources.

When we 'fight' with someone. Whether that fight is physical or a disagreement, how we fight reveals the construct of our own character. A fight, of any type, is an external stressor. Stressors consume our inner resources as we try to deal with them. They also activate our fight or flight response and stimulate our emotions. Emotional regulation depends upon a clear understanding of our aims and goals, our sense of identity and purpose. It is buttressed by our overall behavior.

If those elements are not in place already a sudden, external stressor derails us. Our ability to control the emotional pain we feel, deal with the personal traumas that affect us, solve the issues that arise from them and control our behavior is diminished because we can no longer allocate the resources necessary.

The emotions of the moment then overwhelm us. Our mental filters fail. We react emotionally. And because our emotions have been suppressed, we tend to over-react. In such cases we show the self we have been hiding. We engage in situations that control us instead of us controlling them.

Anne Frank, the Jewish, German-Dutch diarist who died in a German concentration camp during WWII and whose observations made her world famous posthumously also wrote in her diary that was eventually published in *The Diary Of A Young Girl*:

> *"You only really get to know a person after a fight. Only then can you judge their true characters!"*

How we deal with these external stressors is our attitude. Make no mistake here. Unequivocally, the attitude we have is the attitude we want to have. Everything else, emotional pain, physical struggles, material challenges and external stressors can be the result of factors that are completely outside our own control.

Attitude is us. In turn, we become our attitude.

Attitude and Mindset

The entire next chapter is devoted to better understanding how mindset affects who we are and how we can create the mental approach that gets us to be who we want to be. The sole purpose of this section here then is to disambiguate between attitude and mindset. The two are confused, frequently, even by seasoned researchers.

Clarity in what they are and how they affect us provides clarity in what we must do to better control them, so we get the outcomes we want. When we simplify everything to a one-word input so it can become more easily understood and be memorable we run the risk of oversimplification.

Attitude and mindset are the elements that form our interface with the world. Mindset determines how we see the world. Attitude defines how we interact with the world. How we interact with the world however is dependent on how we see it.

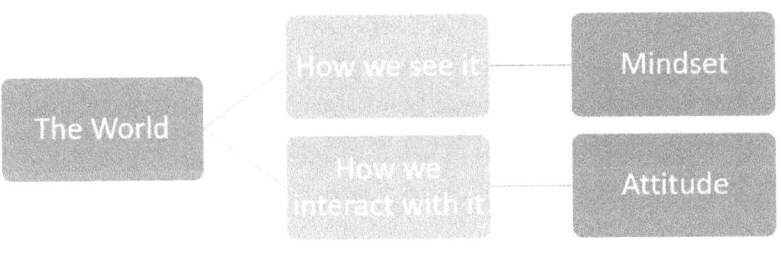

Fig. 9-2 . The way we engage with the world depends both on our mindset and attitude. But before we decide just how to interact with the world we need to define, for our self, how we see it.

If you're a firefighter who believes that a building that is ablaze is too big a fire to put out your decisions, choices and actions as you carry out your job will be different to what they would be if you actually believed that you could put out virtually any building that's on fire.

At this point it is sufficient to say that the mindset we cultivate determines the kind of sense we make of the world. Our attitude then as de Saint-Exupéry said, provides the meaning of things because it leads to actions and actions have both impact and value. Taking action, implies we have come to a decision and made a choice. Choices suggest priorities. Priorities must be based upon some selection process that is guided by our direction in life. A direction generates purpose.

There is a sequential connection between all these and a significant overlap. Specific definitions such as mindset are made up of other elements such as beliefs and perception.

In this complex constellation of cognitive, affective and behavioral traits and attributes attitude stands unique. Not only it is the pinnacle of three specific elements: Cognition, Emotion and Behavior, that require careful moderation to work exactly right and deliver positive outcomes for us, it is also the one specific character modality that, like a snake eating its tale, provides a perfect feedback loop.

The Attitude Paradox

Attitude presents us with a paradox. The way we think, feel and act defines our attitude. But would attitude be absent if we grew up entirely alone, an orphan abandoned by a particularly cruel stork on a desert island? With no one to project to except flora and fauna and no one else for company except our own self would we "lose the attitude" and think, feel, and act in an attitude-free manner?

Apparently not.

Trying to answer the question of whether we would have an attitude if we grew up as the sole inhabitant of a deserted island, psychologist Daryl Bem, who's professor emeritus at Cornell University, ran an experiment in which individuals performing a mundane task were asked to describe it as enthusiastically as possible afterwards while being taped. Listeners were then asked to evaluate and rate the authenticity of the person describing the task. The listeners were divided into two groups. One was told the person on the recording had been paid $1 for his recommendation. The others group was told he'd been paid $20.

The results showed that the listeners rated those who they'd been told had been paid just $1 as being more authentic and credible and they judged they'd truly enjoyed the mundane task they'd been given.

In what has become known as the Self-Perception Theory Bem suggested that our inner world is as opaque to us at times as it is to other people. We then infer our own attitude by observing our actions much as an outside observer infers ours by watching what we do and how we do it.

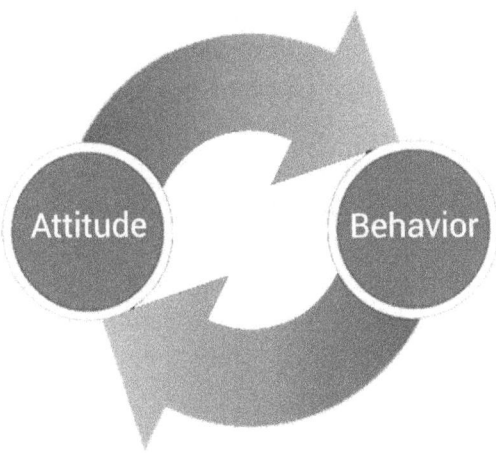

Fig. 9-3. Attitude and behavior form a Yin and Yang-like eternal circle of constant interaction.

Since 1967, which is when Bem ran his experiment, we've had time to better understand how behavioral attributes such as posture and the way we walk and body language and affective traits such as smiling and cognitive attributes such as compartmentalizing our negative moods, affect our behavior by changing our attitude.

To return to my original desert island question, were we to be the totally unsocialized sole inhabitant of that island, we'd still develop an attitude that reflected complex thought processes and our emotional state just by being aware of and analysing our own behavior.

The paradox presented by attitude is that it is in a constant state of readjustment. Our behavior feeds our attitude. Our attitude in turn feeds our behavior. Both are being constantly changed as a result in a Yin and Yang cycle of cause and effect.

The Order Of Things
The attitude paradox begs the question of what do we start off with first? Attitude or behavior? Which should we attribute greater weight to for deeper, lasting, positive change and what should we start off with in order to experience quick, positive results?

This is a chicken-or-the-egg type of question. In 2006 the Walt Disney computer-animated science fiction comedy *Chicken Little* was released on DVD. To drive publicity for its DVD the PR company hired convened a panel comprised of a philosopher, a geneticist and a chicken farmer tasked to solve the question.

In the event, they agreed that the solution required "piecing together the speciation event in which chickens first evolved." The consensus was that the egg came first, a mutation derived from non-chicken parents and giving birth to the world's first genetically recognizable chicken.

In a similar way, the visible part of our attitude is our behavior. Behavior is the manifestation of deeper, underlying neurochemical processes that activate specific mental and emotional states in us and give rise to specific emotions that lead to actions. If we want to dig deep into what makes us tick we need to start with the things we can see first and walk backwards to the things we don't.

Fig. 9-4. Attitude always predates behavior.

If we were simple-minded automatons tasked with creating some sort of rudimentary social system to frame our interactions with each other and visualized our behavior as the sum total of our attitude and intent, we'd be convinced that all we have to do is to change our attitude and totally guide our behavior.

Here is a deeper truth: the context of each one of us is unique. We each unlock different mental, emotional, and psychological resources and respond differently to stimuli. This is true even when the stimulus we each experience is the same. This leads to the realization that we are all, to some degree, lonely. We hunger to connect. We long to be part of something bigger than us. We seek absolute answers to even the most complex of questions because we hope, against hope itself, that they will anchor us in the moment; provide us with a sense of certainty and act as the bulwark against the constant waves of uncertainty and ambiguity that wash over us in every social encounter.

The complex, multi-layered, thickly woven web of our conscious existence is the direct response of the brain trying to help us survive by doing that one 'simple' thing: predicting the next moment.

Subsequent experiments since that early inception of the Theory of Self-Perception in 1967 have shown that our behavior can only partially be inferred by our actions. The caveats here range from the strength of our attitudes (which brings into the frame how there were formed in the first instance), whether our behavior is spontaneous or deliberative and whether our brain calculates that our attitude will increase or decrease the energetic cost we encounter in our decision-making, plus whether our attitudes are explicit and formal or implicit and just implied or generally understood.

There is no denying that attitude is the catalyst to a cascade of neurochemical responses we experience that create the cognitive, affective and behavioral states that make us who we are. By consciously determining our attitude we take control of some of the hidden forces that drive us and take charge of who we want to be.

Even if, at first, we tragically fail to live up to who we want to be; the attitude we exhibit becomes the seed for deeper transformational changes in us which, in time, surface as strong indicators of our behavior and inform our judgement, decisions and choices.

This is the perfect place to finish with a quote from Mark Twain: "What gets us into trouble is not what we don't know. It's what we know for sure that just ain't so." Stay out of trouble.

Points to Remember
- We language to communicate. We also use language to establish our identity and define our capabilities.
- Attitude is the lubricant that reduces the friction we experience as the complex system that is us, fits into the complex system

that is the world.

- Strength of character is the emergent property of attitude.
- The right attitude, cultivated, is a shortcut we can use to obtain positive outcomes.
- Each of us, each day, is engaged in a personal struggle no one else can see.
- Emotional regulation depends on a clear sense on who we are and what our purpose is.
- The attitude we observe in our self is the attitude we *want* to have. It never happens by accident.
- Our attitude is revealed in our actions.
- Loneliness is endemic in our species and, to some extent, unavoidable.

Question Time

- How would you describe your attitude?
- Why do you think it is the way it is?
- What could you do differently to improve it?

Top Tip

- Whenever you feel yourself losing control of your emotions or even when you feel stress and anxiety overwhelm you, focus on taking slow, deep breaths.

10. Mindset

Is a glass filled with water exactly to the halfway mark, half full or half empty? This rhetorical question is more than just sophistry designed to highlight the fragility of our framing when we look at objective reality. Studies show that the way we handle the facts that make up the objective reality around us determines what happens to our physical health and delivers specific outcomes in our personal and professional life.

The way we see the glass of water filled to the halfway mark is our mindset. Our mindset informs our worldview. Our worldview determines our ambitions, hopes, dreams, direction in life. It is reflective of the thoughts, values and beliefs that shape our future.

Would Neil Armstrong have become the first man on the moon if that the age of six he went sailing or horse riding instead of taking an aeroplane flight that set his mind alight with excitement? Would Amelia Earhart have circumnavigated the globe if she had been taught to keep her eyes on the ground all her life and act like patriarchal society thought women were supposed to act in the early 20th century?

Despite its obvious, intuitive power to affect our life the true potential of what the mindset we create can do for us is shrouded in myth and obscured by half-truths. Do a Google search on mindset and dozens of books come up on the subject promising to help you lead a better life, make better decisions, and create a better future for yourself. Prominent, amongst them, Stanford University Psychologist, Carol Dweck's *Mindset* published in 2006 that set off the whole fascination with the subject.

Dweck is rightly influential because her book on the subject dispelled the myth that intelligence and the capabilities of the human brain were fixed upon birth and were only destined to decline throughout a person's life. From her work arose the idea of the "fixed mindset" held by people who believe that the qualities that lead a person to success in life are inborn, fixed, and unchangeable. And the "growth mindset" held by people who believe that these abilities can be developed and strengthened by way of commitment and hard work.

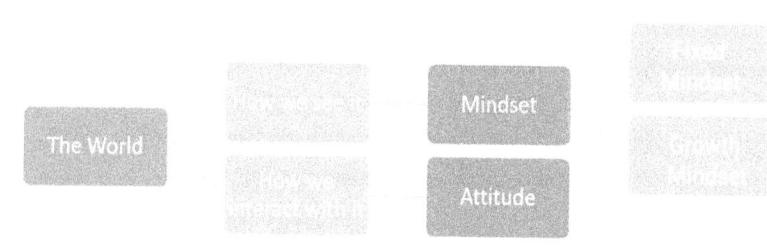

Fig. 10-1. According to psychologist Carol Dweck the mindset we develop is either fixed or growth.

As Dweck writes in her book: "What are the consequences of thinking that your intelligence or personality is something you can develop, as opposed to something that is a fixed, deep-seated trait?" For Neil Armstrong and Amelia Earhart the ability to apply the former over the latter must have made a world of difference but my example is disingenuous. By using two notable outliers I framed the choices in what researchers call "information leakage from logically equivalent frames".

In simpler terms: I framed it so the choice you had when considering whether a fixed or growth mindset is for you offered a choice between two world famous pioneers and abject failure and anonymity. In that regard my implicit bias became your guide and, like a magician on a stage I made you see what I wanted you to see.

The reason I am pulling back the curtain to reveal the mechanics of the sleight of hand I used is not so much to discredit the power of mindset to affect your entire life or to even diminish the impact "fixed" and "growth" mindsets have on us, but to point out the fundamental flaw of mindset books, Dweck's included, that is reflective of a basic trait in us.

Because we are biologically programmed to survive, our brain constantly seeks out shortcuts. Anything that might give us a competitive advantage and promises to deliver a greater return on our investment than the amount of energy we put in lights up our brain and triggers the dopamine spike that makes us feel elated in our discovery.

"Two week diets" that promise us a beach body, several warehouses full of contraptions that promise to reduce our gut and make a six-pack pop while we watch TV, endless arrays of pills, powders, juices and herbal extracts that promise us endless energy and near-instant weight loss, all play on that same desire I just exploited.

I cognitively know that this entire book, in some way, feeds off that very same need to discover a 'secret' that will provide a competitive advantage in life. To possess a 'formula' that can be applied to provide instant success. I have been careful to steer away from this premise by providing facts, ideas and insights that will help you be what you want, on your terms provided you are willing to put in the hard work and dig deep inside you.

In this chapter I will explore further the science behind the mindset theory and how this can be used to our advantage so that we can make better decisions and smarter choices that lead us to the outcomes we want to achieve. But before we get to any of that I will say that the best mindset you can have is to think about and internalize, for yourself, the fact that whatever you want to be, whatever you want to do will always take time and effort, planning and discipline to achieve.

Our past is always in our present. We need to create space for our future by clearing out those things of the past that no longer serve our goals and no longer help our vision.

The best shortcut to remember is that there are no shortcuts.

A Tale Of Two Minds

Google the name "Barbara Oakley" and you'll get stories with titles like "the lit student who became an engineer", "the woman who rewired her own brain", "the professor who learnt how to learn" and hundreds of permutations of these three stories.

Oakley is, indeed, a professor of engineering at Oakland University and McMaster University and the author of several books on learning, mathematics and how to rewire your mind to overcome mental obstacles. She joined the Army, learnt Russian, spent time on Russian fishing trawlers upon being discharged and then came back and trained herself to love mathematics by doing remedial work alongside schoolkids that had failed their year. Along the way, on that journey, she went back to school herself and became an engineer.

If there is a poster child of the growth mindset movement Barbara Oakley has to be it. A person who pulled herself up by her bootstraps each time, just wouldn't accept "cannot" as a definitive answer to her situation and who, in her own words describes her focus and tenacity with: "It's easy to believe that you should only concentrate on subjects that come easily for you. But my story reveals that you can do well in subjects you don't even like."

The thing is that Oakley not only broke free from the mould that keeps soft-science orientated brains from hard-science orientated ones, but she also had to break free from the way 'best' learning is supposed to happen in the process.

Her tale proves that the 'fixed' and 'growth' mindset, rather than being specific values we can ascribe to a person's brain to conveniently sum up their mental capacity are highly dependent upon context. Within every situation, and even perhaps each person, they exist in a fluid spectrum of floating values instead of a specific, fixed point.

Recent studies provide factual evidence for this point by following up decades of educational efforts that tried to shoehorn the growth mindset principles in teaching environments which also faced environmental pressures such as socioeconomic inequality and lack of resources at school level. They showed, conclusively, that despite applying Dweck's learning principles the results they obtained didn't live up to expectation.

Schools in materially deprived areas failed to help their students succeed in life despite pouring a lot of resources in growth mindset teaching principles. Even schools in much better resourced areas failed to show a convincing correlation between growth mindset practises and later success in life.

Dweck, herself, has recently acknowledged the difficulty of blindly applying the principles of growth mindset and expecting them to work. Barbara Oakley, in talking about her journey from top-notch lit student to professor of engineering says how she values both learning by rote and free-thinking as a means of learning anything. Oakley believes we currently underestimate "the Kumon method of teaching mathematics, which emphasizes memorization, repetition, and rote learning hand-in-hand with developing the child's mastery over the material."

What made Oakley capable of the mindshift necessary to go from languages to engineering was the deliberative application of mentalizing, thinking about thinking. She not only was the subject of her 'experiment' undergoing a rigorous course in mental re-training, she was also her own coach. She did all the hard thinking about how to best develop and apply techniques and tactics to help her along her journey. She was her own cheerleader, egging herself on when she flagged and cheering for herself when she did well.

What we learn directly from Oakley's example is that when it comes to the mindset we have, the values we ascribe to the world and the value we ascribe to our self to fit into the world we see, what is important is our own sense of self-worth. Our own sense of capability. Our own capacity to "embrace the suck", as the U.S. Marines say.

Mindset is the product of a sense of agency. Our own identity. If we just accept what is given to us the chances are that we will be forever stuck in the groove someone else has imagined, we belong in. But no one can know us better than we can know our own self.

If you want to break free. If you want to be the most you can be. If you want to be in control of your life and in charge of your choices, you have to be willing to develop the attitude that goes with it You have to be willing to do the boring work, like rote learning, that's not a lot of fun but which helps you develop ingrained skills. To repeat the basketball shot again and again until muscle memory takes over. To accept the difficulty, acknowledge Clausewitz 's concept of "friction" being present in life and still press on.

The take-home message from this then is: It's not what you do. It is the effort it takes to do it, that changes you. The effort needs a reason which means the reason has to have a value which then requires intent. Intent generates focus which allocates attention and the internal resources associated with it. It all then leads towards to something bigger than the need to survive the day. Purpose perhaps. An ideal. A goal that is conceptual instead of tangible.

That is being intentional.

Create Your Own Destiny

In *The Sniper Mind* I wrote: "We cannot learn something new and stick to it without a modular approach to application, positive reinforcement and a real change of environment." I should add to this now, at the very end, "to help us" to complete it.

Basic questions reveal fundamental answers: what creates our mindset? Psychologists say our beliefs. What creates our beliefs? In chapter 6 we saw how expectations and perception play a role and how behavior can both shape and reinforce our belief system.

All of this comes from the brain and the brain is shaped by its very first, impressionable experiences and the sensations it processes from those experiences. Neuroscientists have evidence that our belief in a fixed or growth mindset lies in the structures of the brain and the sense of control of one's life and its destiny that the brain generates as it thinks about things. It stands to reason that the sense of control, as neuroscience sees it, must have a locus; a place where it originates from.

An fMRI study of 777 healthy young adults placed that center of control in the anterior cingulate cortex. The American Psychological Association explains its function as "implicated in a range of executive functions, such as attention allocation, error and novelty detection, working memory modulation, cognitive control, response conflict, and response selection."

The fMRI study carried out by researchers at the University of Fukui, Japan, correlated "white matter volumes in the striatum showed significant correlations with an internal locus of control." In other words, a particular type of structure in the brain, affected the workings of a center that is involved in executive functions and suggested that "cognitive, socioemotional, self-regulatory, and reward systems" are associated with a sense of stronger internal control.

According to this study the belief that one's efforts are rewarded has a strong neuroanatomical basis. This leaves us in a bind. If, indeed, all we will be is the result of who we were and what happened to us in our youth, if the adult of today is the sum total of the child of yesterday up to the age of seven as the Jesuits suggested we can then stop right here, wring our hands, beat our chests and place everything in the hands of destiny, fate and the will of the gods.

In her book *The Science of Fate: Why Your Future is More Predictable Than You Think* University of Cambridge neuroscientist Dr Hannah Critchlow makes the case that it's seductive to think in such terms. In an interview on the subject published in The Guardian she says: "it's a really nice idea, it's a get-out-of-jail card: we are who we are, so we can just rest on our laurels. It's quite reassuring. As a parent, I find it quite comforting for my child, because there are a millions of decisions that

I have to make for him and it's quite nice to think a lot of the work has been done now. The genes, the basic neural circuitry that acts as foundation for his life is already there."

The reality is a little more prosaic. Amongst London cabbies, the passing of the difficult exam that provides them with the license to drive a Black Cab on London's streets and to belong to their very exclusive cab is legendary and, popularly, known as "The Knowledge".

Preparing for the exam is no less gruelling an ordeal than getting through BUDs for a Navy SEAL, though somewhat less physically demanding. For weeks and maybe months prospective cab drivers go through London streets by bicycle, motorbike and on foot, memorizing names and routes, checking out traffic flow and identifying driving conditions, correlating times of day with quickest routes and memorizing potential shortcuts.

When it comes to taking the test that will make them London Cabbies, most fail. The ones who succeed however have managed to rewire their brain and augment their hippocampus. One important role of the hippocampus is to facilitate spatial memory in the form of navigation. In a landmark study published in 2000 "Structural MRIs of the brains of humans with extensive navigation experience, licensed London taxi drivers, were analyzed and compared with those of control subjects who did not drive taxis."

The results showed that "The posterior hippocampi of taxi drivers were significantly larger relative to those of control subjects. A more anterior hippocampal region was larger in control subjects than in taxi drivers. Hippocampal volume correlated with the amount of time spent as a taxi driver (positively in the posterior and negatively in the anterior hippocampus)."

London Cabbies essentially rewire their brain so they can navigate London's labyrinthine streets. A fact that supports their assertion that in the world of cab drivers London Cabbies are in a class of their own.

What we see in this example is no different to what we see in the world of Navy SEALs and their selection process, the SAS and their own unique process for picking likely candidates to join their ranks that is, somewhat unimaginatively called "Selection", or musicians learning to play a repertoire of specific tunes. Namely the rewiring of the brain to deliver performance within a particular context.

Is this a difficult thing to do?

Critchlow, again, says: "It's very difficult. Once you have built up a perception of the world, you will ignore any information to the contrary. Your brain is already taking up about 20% of your energy, so changing the way that you think is going to be quite cognitively costly."

Any energetically costly undertaking requires a clear motivation. This cannot be found without the deep sense of understanding of self that comes from knowing our core values and understanding our core sense of self.

We can all, certainly, let the incidental circumstances of our birth that according to genomic research lay down our neural circuits, guided by our DNA at just 20 weeks' gestation, guide who we become. We can let the behavior of our parents, the expectations of our peers and the unrelenting pressure of our social circles tell us exactly what we can and cannot do, what we should dream about and what we can reach up to.

Or, we can find the reason that will allow us to put in the considerable amount of effort and energy that is required for us to be who we want to be.

In the second film of the *Terminator* franchise Sarah Connor carves with a knife onto the top of a picnic bench the words "No Fate". This is a reminder of the film's message from her son, sent back through time via a human volunteer that says: "The future is not set. There is no fate but what we make for ourselves."

It is uplifting, inspiring and empowering at a deep, intuitive level. It is also highly instructive because even within the structured logic of the film's universe it still takes an enormous amount of energy, effort and focus to change that which is apparently predestined.

The Intentional Mind

The central question of our time is can we, as rational agents, with some degree of awareness of our own mind and some understanding of the complexity of our environment, engage in behavior that is intentional?

As drivers we can safely navigate roads and motorways across the world confident that we are in no danger of dying because everyone around us shares the same rudimentary awareness of the basic rules of driving and no one wants to die.

Every film, fiction book or short story that engrosses us has succeeded to get us to voluntarily suspend disbelief by being able to imagine how we would behave in the situation we are presented with. The amazing point here is that there is no situation that can be imagined that is so unique and so novel that we fail to navigate it with our mind. *Terminator, Sense 8, Sabrina The Teenage Witch, Harry Potter, Lord of the Flies, A Clockwork Orange, Battlestar Galactica, The Firm, To Kill A Mockingbird* and *Catcher In The Rye* represent such a diverse array of themes, ideas and universe-building tropes that it would take a team of PhD candidates to break down, analyze and decipher them all.

Yet, we can all watch them, read them or listen to them and understand completely what they mean, their situation and the specifics of their message without having to break down or even understand the complex background of the socioeconomic, technosocial, quantum-magical or psychodynamic components they contain.

How do we do that?

What is the secret power in our brain that allows us to infer meaning, see mind and understand intent just by witnessing actions and stitching them together even when they are out of sequence?

Cognitive scientist and philosopher, Daniel Dennett, tried to answer this when he postulated his theory of intentional systems. In that, he started by treating each object in the system that interacts with every other object as a unique system, in itself, that is completely rational and can predict the behavior of the systems around it because it assumes (italics mine) that those systems are also rational.

Dennett suggests that we don't really need to know what goes on in other people's heads and behind their eyes but as long as we can be "close enough" with our approximations of their intent to make sense of their behavior, and ours, we don't need to.

Dennett has taken a lot of heat for his theory which fails to take into account the causal aspects of mental states but that is not really our concern here. Dennett's model is sufficiently good for us to consider when we align it with Critchlow's "cognitively costly" task of change.

Our behavior, just like our values, beliefs and motivation is made up of interwoven layers that are not always clear to ourselves, much less to external analysis. Context creates opportunities for contradictions to arise.

We go through life conflicted. Our desire for a cause that will allow us to commit ourselves mind and body to its banner is a cry for clarity in a world that is unclear and a need for certainty in a reality that is fundamentally uncertain.

How we deal with that is what makes us intentional. How we recognize, accept, embrace and then work with our own volatility, fickleness and fragility is what allows us to be consistent, focused and driven.

Without clarity in our thoughts there can be no clarity in our life. But clarity is neither easy to come by nor permanent. As the context of our situation changes, as we change our views, thoughts and priorities, our actions can only be consistent with what is important to us within certain parameters and the imperatives they contain.

Some may take this as a call to justify anything and adopt a "the end justifies the means" approach. That, however, stretches what I just said to the breaking point. A soldier, for instance, is trained to kill but that doesn't automatically turn him into a killer even when operating within parameters where killing is to his direct benefit.

In January 1991 an SAS Patrol using the call sign *Bravo Two Zero*, was dropped behind enemy lines in Iraq during the first Gulf war to gather intelligence on the Iraqi Main Supply Route between Baghdad and North-Western Iraq. Soon after reaching its observation position however the patrol was discovered by a young shepherd and his sheep.

A soldier operating under "the end justifies the means" doctrine would have eliminated that threat and carried out their mission. Instead, the patrol decided to break cover and make a break for it resulting in a chase by armed Iraqi soldiers, who were notified, and the eventual capture of four of the eight men team and the death of three others.

The term "fog of war" is frequently used by soldiers in action to describe the uncertainty in situational awareness experienced by those who take part in armed conflict. Unsurprisingly it was first alluded to and originally introduced as a notion by Carl von Clausewitz, the same child-soldier who went on to be a general in the Prussian Army, write a book called *On War* and give us the notion of friction in daily life when systems interact.

"Fog of war" is the state of heightened uncertainty, elevated perception of threat and a high level of volatility and ambiguity soldiers frequently find themselves operating in. In that state they could, perhaps, justify to themselves and their superiors overreactions that lead to the death of potentially hostile civilians.

To consciously avoid taking such action to the direct and later demonstrable negative impact to their own selves, the men of *Bravo Two Zero* exhibited a heightened degree of clarity of their own values and an awareness of their core beliefs that went beyond the need to survive active deployment.

In seeking clarity, focus, self-awareness, discipline, goal-orientated planning and the ability to self-organize and prioritize we believe that our life will have meaning and we shall be happy. Or, at least, happier.

Certainly all of this makes us feel better about the decisions we take and the choices we make. It gives us a deeper sense of control of our self and a greater sense of awareness of our surroundings and how we fit in them. But happiness, is as misunderstood as many of the other concepts, traits and attributes we've examined here. It is certainly possible to attain. It is even worth actively pursuing to some extent. But it is much more complex than the simple sense of heightened euphoria we commonly associate it with.

Therefore, we examine it last.

Points to Remember

- Mindset is the way we see the world.
- Our past is always in our present. The future we expect won't arrive until we identify and remove the obstacles that hold us back.
- The promise of 'shortcuts' can often blind us to the fact that they are not.
- Without self-awareness we are captive of our past.
- The brain ascribes values to each situation that range from the one extreme of a "fixed mindset" to the other of a "growth mindset".
- Anything we apply blindly fails to deliver what we expect.
- To escape the destiny of our past, we must strive in our present.
- The brain has been creted to see mind and infer meaning.
- We are usually conflicted. Yet we crave its opposite.
- In seeking clarity in our life and meaning in our actions we seek happiness.
- The choices we make and the decisions we take are the life we live.
- Deep down, we all seek a greater sense of control.

Question Time

- Who controls your life now?
- What are the constraints that stop you from living the life you truly want to live?

- Do your beliefs lean towards a fixed or growth mindset?

Top Tip

- Change the actions you undertake that are only meant to gain you the approval of others.

11. Happiness

Never have so many people chased so hard something they don't understand, which means something different to each of them. Chasing happiness is a global obsession. Yet, what truly makes us happy is never what we actively say it is. The disconnect is profound, and it runs deep.

There is a moment, in the 1980 film *Altered States* where the protagonist, played by a young William Hurt, tells his wife about an altered state experience he had while floating in a sensory deprivation tank in his lab. He explains that he'd reverted to being a primal being, virtually feral. He'd hunted, killed and then ate raw a deer to satiate his hunger. "It was a feeling of utter bliss." He recounts, explaining how he felt in that situation. Pure happiness.

This is a Ken Russell film so there are no throwaway lines. Whether by accident or design William Hurt's character defines the psychological definition of happiness. Experiencing directly the sense of relief that comes by meeting the imperatives of survival and their associated rewards.

It is telling that William Hurt's character, in the film, experiences an intense feeling of happiness that arises out of his own actions as a primitive man, driven by basic impulses. The intensity of our feelings drives our actions even when we have trouble articulating what it is exactly that we feel. It takes a truly intentional approach to being to determine when we should give in to our emotions and when we should modulate them. Unsurprisingly then, when it comes to modern human happiness we are presented with a paradox.

On the one hand we seem to constantly pursue happiness. A Google search for "How to be Happy" brings up 4.7 billion pages in the results while a search for "Why Am I Unhappy" (as a counterbalance) barely makes the 109 million mark. There are even online courses on how to be happy, some 642 million of web pages offering them in one form or another and let's not forget the core focus of the positive psychology movement now almost seventy years old whose aim at reinforcing "positive experiences" is just another name for happiness.

On the other hand, we seem to be genetically programmed to avoid happiness. A brain whose one-line dictate is meant for us to physically survive cannot but be inherently suspicious of any prolonged feeling that makes us feel content and relaxed. Willing to extend trust towards others and our surroundings and lower our guard against threats. This makes our feeling of happiness, even when we do manage to attain it, transient by design.

We couldn't have designed a more ambivalent response to an internal state we experience had we consciously tried to find a way to hamper our own development and handicap our every effort for internal and external progress.

The perception of the importance of happiness to who we are and who we end up becoming is deep enough to have manifested itself on the 2nd August 1776. In what was to become the United States of America, the Founding Fathers got together to sign the Declaration of Independence.

The second paragraph of the first article of the United States Declaration of Independence starts with:

"We hold these truths to be self-evident, that all men are created equal, that they are endowed by their Creator with certain unalienable Rights, that among these are Life, Liberty and the pursuit of Happiness."

The fact that in the US alone there is an industry worth eleven billion dollars a year that revolves around the pursuit of happiness and positive experiences suggests that two and half centuries later we still are no nearer to making happiness easy to attain.

But why are we like that? Why is happiness so elusive to us? Other basic needs such as hunger, thirst and sex are much easier to satisfy even if the state of satisfaction is also transient. Our civilization has created massive utilities designed to meet the demands of the first two and complex social rituals that fulfil the third. In the same vein, by now, we should have in place ways and means through which we would be happier.

When, overall, we are free from the anxiety of basic survival. When our health is not in immediate danger and our life is not directly threatened, we should be positioned ideally to deliver on something we all so intensely desire. Yet happiness appears to be eluding us. Our best efforts to attain it clearly fail to deliver.

Whenever something appears elusive despite our best efforts it is usually because we are either missing something vital in our approach or our approach is flawed. Maybe we are failing to correctly articulate the problem we are trying to solve or maybe the problem we are trying to solve is not the problem we should be solving.

Ironically, when it comes to the question of what is it that makes us happy there are many interested parties that would really love to know the answer.

Employers across the globe would love to have happy employees. One productivity study after another has produced incontrovertible data that show happy workers are self-driven, focused and deliver higher quality work. School teachers across the globe know that happy students learn faster and retain more of what they have learnt. Governments know that happy citizens generate a greater gross domestic product for the country, cause fewer socio-political issues and exercise greater initiative in their civic duty.

I would personally love nothing more to just be able to put a one-line formula here which would allow you to close the final pages of this book, put it into effect and experience a state of inner bliss forever.

Now, if you think that my wish sounds weird because, intuitively, you feel that no such formula could exist and. You are right. From personal experience alone you must know that the states of happiness you have experienced vary in circumstances and intensity. That knowledge should be enough to alert you to the fact that there can be no one-line formula that will work. Yet were I to advertise that there can be, the number of readers who'd respond would likely allow me to buy myself a small island.

So, I am doing myself a disservice in not advertising my book this way, harming both potential sales and royalties I would receive. But here's the thing, which perfectly illustrates the conundrum of happiness. Had I done that and falsely advertised my book this way and enjoyed the kind of sales that delivered a few million copies, I wouldn't be happy.

If anything, having lied to my readers, I'd be feeling anxious, stressed and would be looking for ways to make up for what I would see as a serious dereliction of my duty as a writer. Happiness then is a subjective internal state. It partially arises out of the synthesis of who we are, our sense of purpose, our values and our understanding of how we fit in the world.

The happiness industry and even some psychologists want us to believe that happiness is a choice. Neuroscience and neurobiology correlate happiness to specific neurophysiological states, the activation of specific neural centers in the brain and the function of specific neurotransmitters. Philosophers have forever told us that happiness is physical (i.e. hedonism) and emotional and psychological (i.e. eudaimonia). Anyone who's ever been to a party that got out of hand is familiar with the former while the latter is usually preserved as an internal reward for those who "lead a good life".

With so many competing definitions for happiness and, indeed, so many different fields of expertise vying to tell us how to be happy it is no surprise that we fail to understand what happiness is. At the same time popular culture and relentless advertising have convinced us to engage in an ever-intensifying pursuit of it.

The Choice Of Being Happy

As a thought experiment, suppose, you managed to put everything in the first ten chapters of this book to immediate and highly effective use. Would that make you happy? Would a greater awareness of your own inner workings and a deeper knowledge of how the outside world works help you feel better about yourself and your choices?

If the answer is no, would that then qualify as a personal failing? A choice you didn't make?

That is the core problem with the choice of happiness.

The other problem associated with happiness lies in how we see it. Far too often being happy is farmed to an external source or event because it presents us with a tangible point of data we can analyze and quantity. When we are on holiday, for instance, we feel relaxed and carefree. The novelty of our surroundings plus, maybe, the novelty of our carefree, stress-free situation deliver a dopamine spike that activates our reward system and makes us feel good and want more of it.

We may seek, as a result, holidays as our source of happiness. By the same mechanism we may seek to buy a new pair of shoes we don't really need, a new coat when we have more than one already, new T-shirts, new relationships, or a new cell phone when the one we have is perfect for our needs.

External factors enamour us with their novelty. That novelty soon wears off, however.

If all we have are external factors we soon find ourselves locked into a pattern of behavior that chases an ever-elusive state that is never meant to last. There is a lot to unpack here so let's start peeling back the layers.

The Chemical States Of Happiness

From a neurochemical point of view happiness is relatively easy to explain. We feel a state of euphoria when our brain experiences a surge of dopamine (popularly called the motivation hormone), serotonin (sometimes called the lead hormone) and oxytocin (called the trust hormone). The presence of these hormones in our brain triggers a number of neurobiological responses which then lead to physiological changes: our breathing, blood pressure and body temperature become more even. Our metabolic system works more smoothly. We feel at peace with the world. Our stress levels drop. And our willingness to interpret the intentions of others as benign increases.

This neurochemically induced level of physical wellbeing is unlikely to last long. It's a little bit like an orgasm during sex. The orgasmic state during sexual intercourse in humans is marked by an increase in dopamine that activates the reward system in the brain, rising levels of serotonin that enhances pleasure, oxytocin that leads to trust and bonding with another person and noradrenaline that accelerates some physical responses. When we do reach orgasm however all these chemical states that present us with a peak sensation of physical pleasure, subside.

What we feel next however takes us from the realm of physical and, evidently, primal sensations to the realm of thoughts, beliefs and values. Our after-sex state of being depends on where we are inside our head and how we see ourselves in the world.

Even after great, consensual sex, statistics show that almost half of the population will, at some point, feel sad and depressed. This is a state that neurobiological researchers call post-coital dysphoria and studies have shown that forty-six per cent of women and forty-one per cent of men will experience it at least once in their lifetime. Having ridden the rollercoaster of sensations and emotions of sexual intercourse to a peak we must now, it seems, let it take us into a trough. This makes sense because intense emotions or prolonged emotions deplete the brain's neurochemical stores and until they are replenished, we are stuck at the bottom of a proverbial barrel.

Ending up at the bottom of that barrel however is not inevitable. Studies show that fifty-four per cent of the population never experiences this state of being despite having just as emotionally satisfying and physically intense sexual intercourse. The difference between those who do end up lying in bed afterwards feeling a certain amount of what can only be described as regret and those who do not, lies in a complex mix of psychology and cognition, expectations and beliefs.

Religion, morality, memories, past experiences, and underlying physical issues play a role in the experience of post-coital dysphoria. A similar mix of psychological, cognitive and physical factors also play a role in the happiness we experience in any other moment in our life and its aftermath.

To illustrate this better, let's play a thought experiment: You are given a million dollars on the proviso that it must all be spent on your birthday party. You would think that with that kind of money to throw at a personal event that is usually associated with positive emotions, you will be able to throw a birthday party that will be memorable in every way and elicit highly positive feelings.

The odds are however that any memorability produced here will of the negative sort. A party this costly has huge logistical issues: stage, food, decorations, entertainment, venue. Organizing that, even if you just pay someone to do it, produces high levels of anxiety and worry.

The party then needs to be appreciated so you really want to invite as many people as you can, and you then need to exceed their expectations and satisfy them all completely. Suppose that you are so conscientious and meticulous in your planning that you spend every available waking moment, for weeks, on it and it goes off without a single hitch.

Would you be happy?

You might be satisfied having pulled off a really hard task, but happiness requires other things. Your stress levels leading up to it, the overall involvement in every tiny detail, the micro-managing and the problem-solving required plus the fact that there is a perfectly acceptable, low-key alternative where you and some close friends get together at a pub, would conspire to rob you of feeling happy. And, on top of it, is the serious likelihood of the whole thing feeling like an anti-climax. Weeks and weeks of grind, planning, thinking, and solving being over in just a few hours.

What this tells us about the neurochemical state of happiness is that it is defined by a balance between our efforts and rewards, expectations and beliefs, feelings, and thoughts. And it is up to us to engineer it.

Engineering happiness is different from choosing it. Engineering is a process we put into motion to produce a specific intent. Choosing is deciding. No one decides to be unhappy. By the same logic no one can just decide to be happy.

Happiness Is An Effort

In *Striking Thoughts*, a book of collected Bruce Lee aphorisms that reflect his philosophy for life, the iconic martial artist and actor says: "We should devote ourselves to being self-sufficient and must not depend upon the external rating by others for our happiness."

In exploring this state of mind, Bruce Lee was doing what he had been attempting to do most of his adult life: Analyze and quantify the elements that contribute to specific emotional states which then prompt the body to take action.

That Lee sought to better understand happiness is no surprise. We all do this, even if we do not openly admit it. Field researchers report that the quest for happiness cuts across countries, ages, and cultures. It seems to also cut across time. If we all, reportedly all the time, seek to be happy what is it exactly that we seek to attain?

Obviously not novelty. That soon gets tiring. Certainly not a sated state of bliss, like the primitive sensation of the protagonist of *Altered States*. That never lasts and, at any rate, it is purely sensory in nature. Even a perfectly balanced neurochemical state is not happiness. It is hard for us to determine so it cannot be actively pursued, and it is, by nature, destined to be ephemeral. The moment the body attains any kind of balance in its neurochemical status the external world intervenes to upset it.

Bruce Lee wrote about devoting our self to attaining happiness which sounds like this requires effort. Effort is certainly key to it but effort alone, blindly applied, is about as useless as blindly applying grit and we have already seen how that fails to work as expected.

Happiness then is not a choice; it obviously isn't a perfectly balanced neurochemical state and it isn't something to be purely found in external actions and external factors. The effort Bruce Lee mentions, to work, needs to be applied to specific targets within specific boundaries. It takes everything we covered so far, Identity, Goals, Motivation, Behavior, Beliefs, Values, Grit, Attitude and Mindset to emerge, provided we strive for it in a deliberative, self-aware manner.

It seems ridiculous that happiness; the thing we all seek so desperately requires so much effort, knowledge, and application to occur. This, I suggest, is because happiness just like consciousness, is an emergent phenomenon. It appears when a lot of other things have taken place and function properly. The American Psychological Association's definition of consciousness that it is "an organism's awareness of something either internal or external to itself." But the APA struggles with its definition, like everyone else, expanding it to include so much that it eventually can mean anything. Adding caveats all along the way.

By comparison, the APA definition of happiness sounds equally terse and truncated: "an emotion of joy, gladness, satisfaction, and well-being."

How we recognize either happiness or consciousness is still a tricky question to answer for experts. Field researchers avoid it because each time they try to define it context wrongfoots them. Professional organizations that provide the umbrella under which psychologists or neuroscientists work, admit that broad definitions are meaningless and focus on specifics. When it comes to happiness they use self-reporting of a state of happiness or the identification of the activation of neural substrates that represent distinct mental states. In this way happiness can be represented in field reports and studies but all of this skirts the issue of what exactly it is that is being represented.

If happiness, just like consciousness, is an emergent phenomenon what is that it emerges out of? Why does effort, striving in effect, make it possible for happiness to emerge?

I have some answers here.

The Stepping Stone To Happiness
A YouGov survey in 2016 asked Americans would they rather "achieve great things or be happy?" More than eight out of ten, a full eighty-one per cent, said they'd rather choose to be happy. Yet, just fifty-one per cent of those surveyed in a 2020 survey reported wanting to lose weight and be healthier.

The disparity is significant, and it feeds into the general disconnect that exists between our virtually obsessive, universal pursuit of happiness and our understanding of what it is we want to attain to be happy.

This is an important point to make. You would think, in a book about being intentional in your life, being intentional in your pursuit of happiness is exactly what's required but that is not how it works. As an emergent phenomenon happiness emerges only when other conditions are met. Just like you cannot just conjure up creativity into existence and make it manifest itself at will in a brainstorming session (an example I have, sadly, seen in action), so you cannot just will yourself to be happy or arbitrarily decide that happiness is the lack of something material that you just need to attain.

Advertising, marketing and our own sense of hope for easy solutions to our complex problems conspire against us in this. Happiness, we believe, is going to be found in our next purchase. Happiness is a 'thing' that is out there waiting for us to somehow, magically, get to it and grasp it. If we don't yet possess it because we feel unhappy, we tell ourselves that we need to find where it is and then just go out and buy it or possess it.

Happiness, as it turns out, is a lot closer to home. Its foundation, the central building block it rests upon, is inside our body and it expresses itself through good health. Countless field studies have linked feeling happy with overall higher levels of health and well-being. A state of happiness has an undeniable correlation with the expression of positive neurochemical states and physiological events in the body. The neurochemical states and physiological events that correlate to happiness however absolutely cannot occur without a healthy body and a healthy brain.

New Age speaker and writer, Deepak Chopra, frequently opens his presentations by stressing how "The mind is not in the brain. It is everywhere." Our expanding knowledge of the central nervous system and the way the brain processes information has led us to discover that there are 40,000 neurons in the heart that process information, learn and remember. In addition, "the heart communicates with the brain in many methods: neurologically, biochemically, biophysically, and energetically."

There are an additional two hundred to six hundred million neurons lining the gut, using "a new set of pathways that use gut cells to rapidly communicate with … the brain stem." The gut communicates with the brain via hormones but the neurons lining it also use electrical signals and "glutamate, a neurotransmitter involved in smell and taste, which the vagal neurons picked up on within 100 milliseconds—faster than an eyeblink."

The heart and the gut are key components of the overall systemic health of the complex, nested system that is an individual.

We can see this when problems occur in the communication of the gut with the brain, perhaps due to gastroenteric issues or because of medication, like appetite depressants, that suppress the gut neuron action. This disruption in communication between the neural networks of the gut and the brain has been linked to the onset of depression and even the development of dementia later in life.

Clearly, we cannot begin to talk about happiness without taking into account a sense of identity, focus and purpose. None of these qualities can emerge when we are battling bad physical health and are mentally struggling to make sense of our life.

If happiness is an emergent phenomenon, which increasingly looks like it is, then everything else must align to some degree for us to experience it in a consistent and sustainable way. Chopra makes a similar point when he says that "the brain and the body are not structures, they are processes."

But processes cannot be initialized if the vessel within which they take place is damaged.

John Stuart Mill, for example, shaped the bulk of early 19th century political economy and social theory and the development of classical liberalism. In his writings he considered "that happiness is desirable, and the only thing desirable, as an end". Ironically, Mill himself, was unable to experience pleasure of any kind, much less happiness because he was a damaged vessel.

Neuroscientists and psychologists, today understand that Mill suffered from anhedonia. A neuropsychiatric condition that has been identified as a core feature of major depressive disorder, the definition of the melancholic subtype. Anhedonia, which affects motivation and, by direct association, goal setting, can be treated through medical intervention that is now part of a growing expertise in neuropharmacology.

Treating the physical being to cure cognitive or psychological disorders is only part of the equation. Nevertheless, it remains a widely acknowledged and scientifically supported truth that without healthy physical and neural substrates it becomes difficult to experience the full range of feelings and emotions that make us complete, fully functioning human beings.

Formalizing the link between physical health and psychological well-being a recent longitudinal study published in the *Journal of Behavioral Medicine* followed more than 18,000 middle-aged and older men and women over a period of eight years. The study showed that those who had a strong purpose in life at the start of the study were more likely to engage in exercise and those who exercised were more likely to report feeling a stronger sense of purpose in life.

This direct bi-directional correlation was then observed in a separate longitudinal study following nearly 14,000 adults over five years and it was further borne out by a review of thirteen cross-sectional studies and two other longitudinal studies plus eight intervention studies all of which, again, showed the direct relationship between self-reported feelings of happiness and exercise.

The scientific hypothesis to account for this states that physical activity provides a sense of goals and achievement which then reinforces the circuits in the brain that deal with planning and goal setting and activates the reward system which receives a dopamine spike each time a sense of achievement is felt.

As a result, the brain circuits that create motivation are exercised. The neural centers of the brain involved in executive decision making, emotional regulation, planning, goal setting and prioritization also get used to being routinely activated. All this neural activity makes it easier for the brain to activate the same neural circuits in other, non-physical activity related situations. The phenomenon where a particular ability or skillset is transferred from one situation where it takes place to another with a different context is called, in psychology, transfer.

Consumers of popular culture will recognize the principal of transfer used in the fictional Mr. Miyagi's teaching technique in the 1984 hit *The Karate Kid*. In teaching Daniel LaRusso to "wax on, wax off" as he tasks him to wash and wax his car, he's basically teaching him how to fight and take care of himself by developing physical coordination, balance and timing.

Just like in the film itself however, transfer is not automatic. It requires an awareness of the skill possessed and an understanding of its value in the fresh context before it can be applied. In *The Karate Kid* movie Mr Miyagi has to explain to a disenchanted Daniel the value of the skills he has acquired through seemingly meaningless tasks of washing and waxing his teacher's car. Before I wrote my book, *The Sniper Mind*, I interviewed hundreds of combat veterans who were capable of exercising initiative, innovative thinking, resource and skill prioritization, goal setting, planning and organization skills in the battlefield but then, when they were out of the army, felt they had no skillset that could be useful to a business.

Self-awareness takes stock of what we have and reappraises the value of our skillset in each context. But it requires a readjustment of our sense of identity and purpose in life. Self-awareness is central to assessing our own capabilities and, once we do, feeling confident in what we can do. Confidence, in turn, contributes significantly to our sense of control over our life. A sense of control is what allows us to critically examine and adjust our beliefs, hold firm to our core values, develop the right kind of attitude and display grit when we need it.

Intuitively, we understand that if we feel these emotions and feelings and implement these traits and attributes in the small-scale context of physical activity, we can then exercise them in the much broader context of situations that make much greater demand of cognition and emotional intelligence, decision-making and emotional regulation.

So, start small. Get physical. Be consistent. Understand the why before you get to the what. And feel what you do. And, enjoy the moment.

Happiness Is An Experience

In a pivotal scene in the first of *The Matrix* trilogy of films Joe Pantoliano who plays Cypher, negotiates the terms of his betrayal of his friends with Agent Smith (played by Hugo Weaving) by saying: "I don't want to remember nothing. Nothing. You understand? And I want to be rich. You know, someone important. Like an actor."

Cypher's take on the importance and relevance of actors aside, what is important to us now is the fact that he was asking to be reinserted into the Matrix because it was going to make him feel happier than the way he was feeling outside it. And central to that happiness he expected to experience was his inability to remember his betrayal and the life he had before he sold out his friends.

Memory and expectation are key to our sense of happiness. One of the reward pathways in the brain is the mesolimbic pathway. It transmits dopamine signals from the nerves in the middle of the brain to the limbic system and the prefrontal cortex. It also plays an important role in the storage of memories and learning.

We can't decide what action to take without first understanding the context of a situation. When our expectations are not being met our brain reaches for past experiences to guide us. What we know, what we have experienced, what we have learnt and what we remember then becomes vital to our experience of happiness.

Cypher's characters in *The Matrix* perfectly understood that or, at the very least, felt it sufficiently for him to ask for his memory of his despicable conduct to be erased.

Observable behavior has a foundation in less observable mental calculations that determine how we manage uncertainty, probable outcomes, expected rewards and foreseen consequences. The mathematical name for that is "Bayesian Computation through Cortical Latent Dynamics" and it basically means that when we do not directly understand something we rely on a complex mental calculus that takes statistical regularity as its cornerstone.

This is how it works in practice: If going out, getting drunk and hooking up with someone for a night made us happy in the past and we are now experiencing a state of unhappiness which we don't know how to change, the chances are that we shall reach for that past behavior in the expectation that since it worked in the past, it will do so again.

We use the remembered reliability of our experience of the past to navigate the uncertainty of the future via actions in the present. The way we access our experience of the past is through memory. In assessing a situation we encounter our brain focuses on the past, as an anchor, the present, for current sensory input, and the future for threat detection.

As we shall see, this splitting of our attention and the mental and psychological resources associated with it have severe implications for our ability to experience happiness. Before we get to it at the end of this chapter though, it serves us well to examine a little more closely how we experience happiness through experience.

Two very recent studies that, collectively, looked at over 3,000 adults and mapped their response to direct experiences, experimentally proved something that theorists have been surprisingly agreeing on since 1737 when the Scottish philosopher David Hume suggested it. Namely that spending money on experiences makes us happier than spending money on possessions.

The first study, catchingly titled *Spending on doing promotes more moment-to-moment happiness than spending on having* tracked 2,635 adults as they made purchases which they would then were asked to grade in how happy it made them. To serve as a control group, a further 5,000 participants were then recruited whose mood was tracked first and then were quizzed about whether they had made a purchase prior to being quizzed about their mood.

The results revealed that those who had purchased an experience consistently reported greater levels of happiness over those who had made a material purchase even when the material purchase was used frequently. Purchasing an experience always resulted in greater self-reported happiness even when compared with material purchases made by the same person.

The second study was smaller in scale. *Titled Happiness for Sale: Do Experiential Purchases Make Consumers Happier than Material Purchases?* recruited over 500 students from different campuses who were then incentivized to recall and rate in detail their experience over a material or an experiential purchase.

As expected the study validated expectations. Experiential purchases provided greater, overall, levels of happiness over material ones, but counterintuitively it also showed that when the experience was negative the experiential purchase produced greater negative feelings than the material purchase.

The disparity however is better explained when we take into account how memory works and its key role in happiness. Material purchases may produce a jolt of happiness due to their novelty but that soon wears off. In addition, frequent use induces habituation. We simply stop noticing them that much and they fade into the background of our awareness.

Experiences however are more engaging by definition. They activate a much broader neural network in the brain, and they are incorporated into the narrative that forms the micro-moments of our life. In that regard a bad experience will always be more vividly remembered and more easily recalled over a bad product. That however doesn't necessarily mean it makes us unhappy even if we may report it as such.

To understand the contradiction, consider how many times you've recounted a bad experience you had with friends, over dinner or drinks, turning what was a negative impact at the time into a good story that delivers social status dividends.

Because experiences are, by definition, less rigid in structure than a product they also engage to a much greater degree our anticipation and participation than any product could hope to.

No matter how broad a prescriptive approach we adopt for happiness it will always appear elusive and hard to replicate universally. It relies on the satisfaction of specific conditions that are created out of the unique combination of the context of our situation, our expectations, anticipation, and engagement within the moments our awareness perceives.

That hasn't stopped purveyors of instant fixes to try and deliver a happiness equation.

The Happiness Equation

Harvard psychologist Daniel Gilbert, in his book, *Stumbling on Happiness*, suggests that our social 'instinct' and the brain's pro-social behavior are behind our sense of happiness. This makes the relationships we form and the relationships we maintain the primary sources for our source of happiness, which reinforces the idea that happiness stems from experiences rather than single-point events that focus on an instance or a thing.

Gilbert's supposition is that relationships help us make sense of the world and safeguard us against adversity. Because we prioritize some over others and intentionally choose to reinforce some ties while letting others become weaker, we create the support network we need to deliver positive interactions and improved experiences.

Harvard MBA, Neil Pasricha, in his book, *The Happiness Equation*, provides an instant, if somewhat new-age derivative fix with the subtitle: *Want Nothing + Do Anything=Have Everything*. Despite the gimmicky subtitle Pasricha breaks down his formula into what can be summarized as the 4Ss of Social, Structure, Stimulation and Story.

The social aspect of our lives features heavily in any work that takes a serious look at what makes us happy. It is to be expected, as we acquire our values and test our beliefs through prosocial learning and we use the social component of our life to understand how to best behave in each situation.

Structure is about planning and prioritizing while Stimulation is about engagement which, as we saw in chapter five, partially stems from passion in what we do. Story is, of course, about narrative and how it fits into our sensemaking and identity-curation activities.

If all of the above sound a little more involved than you might expect this is because nothing that has to do with happiness is easy. Providing a seemingly simpler fix perhaps is Google engineer, Mo Gawdat, whose book, *Solve for Happy: Engineer Your Path to Joy* attempts to shoehorn spiritualism and practical psychology into a handy approach for overcoming personal adversity. Gawdat, got to this stage by having to overcome deep personal loss so his book and its journey is deeply personal and that is reflected in his solution. Gawdat says that happiness is greater than, or equal to, your perception of the events in your life minus your expectation of how life should be. Again, expectation, perception and, inevitably, experiences and memory are the ingredients through which happiness can arise.

Finally, I close this section with Martin Seligman, proponent of positive psychology and founder of the Positive Psychology Centre at the University of Pennsylvania. Seligman's formula for happiness is very similar to Gawdat's with a little more formalism thrown in. It goes like this: $H=S+C+V$, where happiness (H) is the sum of a person's genetic capacity for happiness (S), their circumstances (C), and factors under their voluntary control (V).

It's intuitive enough to be grasped without deeply understanding its particulars. Of everything we looked at here it is also, arguably, the one that best sums up the nexus point between person, environment and the world.

Happiness has a physical foundation. Both Gawdat and Seligman make that point. We've already seen that each of us is a complex system that has to fit, imperfectly, into the greater system that is the world. The interaction generates friction. This is the difficulty we experience in just getting through life. Now imagine trying to deal with that friction and make headway with a system that's buggy due to ill health.

The difficulties you face will be exponential.

Happiness Is A Diamond

So far, the happiness equation we all seek is the result of good health, exercise, helping others, identity, purpose, engagement with reality, seeking experiences over purchasing things, good memory and managed expectations.

Happiness is complicated because, just like a diamond, it appears to present a different facet whichever way you turn it to examine it. It is all of the things I mentioned above but not for everyone. Some people need to have them all to feel happy. Others need just one, or two items from the list.

One of the most prolific, recent, explorers in the neuroscientific study of happiness has been Robb Rutledge who receives funding from his research from the National Institute of Mental Health, the Medical Research Council, and the Brain & Behavior Research Foundation.

Using mobile phones and a game app to explore momentary happiness and, also, the longer aftermaths of it he and his team studied 18,420 people to better understand what it is that actually makes them happy. His findings indicate that momentary happiness depends on our experience of learning and making progress and our own personal set of expectations.

Rutledge pinpoints expectations as of particular importance. High expectations tend to spoil the happiness we might feel at a positive outcome that somehow, falls a little short of what we expected. This is exactly the ground covered by my one million dollars to throw a birthday party thought experiment, earlier in this chapter.

Another telling result of Rutledge's research is that while his subjects reported happiness at a particular events and outcomes none of them seemed to be able to feel happy for long, afterwards. This, Rutledge says is suggests that "time-limited joy is an adaptation that helps your brain adjust to your circumstances, so you are ready to make your next move."

Happiness is ephemeral by design. Were we to attain pure, eternal bliss we might end up dying soon, blindsided by a threat we failed to perceive as we basked in our deep sense of happiness and we will most certainly fail to progress as motivation is the movement from a state of unhappiness or dissatisfaction to a place of greater happiness or satisfaction.

The transient nature of happiness and its highly personal tone doesn't mean we should stop looking for ways to formulaically generate it. Quite the opposite in fact. As Rutledge says in one his studies "The subjective well-being or happiness of individuals is an important metric for societies." The future of our civilization does actually hang on our capacity to generate happiness not just for our self but also for those around us.

Happiness Is A Process

As an emergent phenomenon the happiness we experience is the result of the choices we make, the decisions we take and the actions we engage in. The most accurate way to describe happiness is to say that it is a process of becoming. An experience of the sum of the transitions that take us from one moment to the next.

It is a skill to be able to find joy in ordinary things and to experience the wonder of being alive in everyday events. In this context each moment is experienced fully. But living in the moment doesn't mean coping out and failing to plan. Nor does it mean living in a way that doesn't look to the future or does not remember the past. After all we need anticipation and planning and learning and memory to function properly.

We all live in two worlds, one on either side of our skin. We need to be able to fully function in both of them to feel happy. When anxiety, worry and the weight of the uncertainty we face as we contemplate the future overwhelm us our mental and physical health suffer. Our mental and psychological resources are insufficient to help us keep things together. We become lost to ourselves, unable to see our place in the future. If we can't see our place in the future the odds are that we've lost our sense of place in the present.

When we are absorbed by worry and anxiety our brain seeks to protect itself by diving into the past. A truly happy person can live fully in the moment without excluding the future from sight or forgetting the past.

In writing *Intentional* I set out to chart the steps required to live an intentional life. To help you make choices you want to make, fully aware of their cost and their impact so you can control the outcomes they deliver and have a more fulfilling life.

In the process I came to realize that happiness can no more be chased than it can be bought. But it can be experienced.

I will close this chapter with one final thought: Happiness like creativity is not diminished if you share it. It is affected by external factors but it also depends on them. It emerges when our focus is not in seeking happiness but in improving our sense of identity, in reaching specific goals, in experiencing learning that broadens our perspective of the world. It appears when we least expect it when we forget about our self and focus on how to best help others, how to reduce the friction they experience as they too try to make themselves fit in the world.

Ultimately, each of us is responsible for discovering our own happiness, but happiness, a supremely personal emotion, evaporates in the face of selfishness. In a world where each of us only takes care of himself, we all feel the friction. We grate against the world and we grate against each other. Nothing is ever easy. Things, arguably, only ever become harder.

If happiness emerges from our experience of becoming who we want to be, if it arises as we go about our journey through life when our focus on what we do helps us reach a place where we can feel the impact of our actions then this makes us co-responsible for the happiness of those around us.

It is hard to accept that we are responsible for how others feel. The moment we do however it changes everything. And it changes us.

Points to Remember
- From a neuroscientific point of view happiness is a neurochemical and neurobiological relief from discomfort.
- Happiness, as a concept, is not clearly understood. Nor is it clearly defined in scientific literature.
- Neurochemically we feel happy when we experience a sustained dopamine spike that activates the brain's reward system.
- We cannot just choose to be happy but we can engineer the process that helps us experience happiness.
- Happiness is an emergent phenomenon.
- Memory helps happiness materialize.
- Experiences create happier memories than material purchases.
- Happiness is highly personal and multi-faceted. It relies on learning about the environment. Memory. Past experiences. Expectations.

Question Time
- When was the last time you felt truly happy?
- When was the last time you made someone else truly happy?
- How do you define happiness?

Top Tip
- Take a picture of a flower. Photograph a sunset. Perhaps find a

song or a poem that deeply resonates with you. Find for yourself the beauty in what you see. Think about how it makes you feel inside yourself. Share some of the things you find joy in with others.

Appendix 1 – The Kanizsa Illusion And The Way Perception Is Formed

Psychologists define perception as:

> *"the process or result of becoming aware of objects, relationships, and events by means of the senses, which includes such activities as recognizing, observing, and discriminating. These activities enable organisms to organize and interpret the stimuli received into meaningful knowledge and to act in a coordinated manner."*

The way we process the information our senses receive and create a representation of our environment is critical to our surviving. Yet our brain, trying to conserve computing power and, at the same time, guess the next moment to aid in our survival, creates shortcuts that enable us to see things that don't exist. Sometimes this is beneficial. We can guess a child is about to run into the street ahead of us by seeing a football rolling across the road. At other times it can be detrimental. By refusing to accept coincidence as a reason our brain latches onto conspiracy theories as an explanation.

The Kanizsa Triangle illusion we saw in Chapter 6 was created by Italian psychologist Gaetano Kanizsa in 1955. In gestalt psychology the illusion is used to describe the law of closure which states that "individuals perceive objects such as shapes, letters, pictures, etc., as being whole when they are not complete. Specifically, when parts of a whole picture are missing, our perception fills in the visual gap." In advertising the Coca Cola bottle with its distinct shape has used it extensively to subliminally engage audience participation for the bran by frequently presenting it incomplete.

Participation leads to engagement of mental resources which lead to an increase in the affective impact of the brand. The way the Kanizsa illusion works is be letting the brain perceive a triangle where no triangle actually exists by filling the whole from what we think are parts. So, we readily perceive three black circles and two triangles, even though there are technically no circles or triangles in the image.

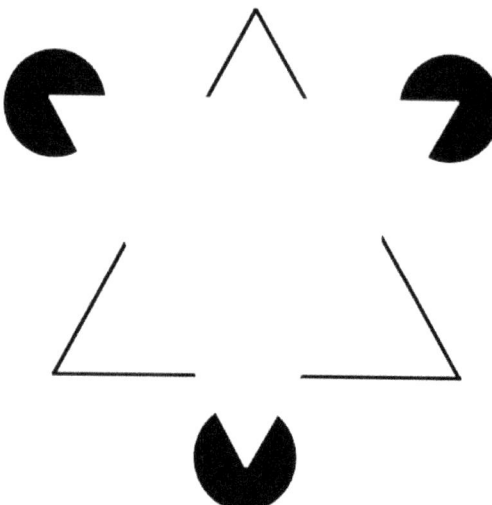

Psychologists agree that the illusion challenges the reductionist approach to vision as what we see in the image is not merely the sum of all its parts. We see something more. "We actually perceive objects that are not really there."

Kanizsa, in his 1955 explanation of the phenomenon drew a distinction between modal and amodal completion of contours. In modal completion, he explained, the brain creates a visual experience of an object that is not there by experiencing edges that are created by contrast, color or luminance. In the Kanizsa triangle the triangle that one seems to see pointing upwards is a classic example of modal completion.

The triangle that, in the illustration, seems to be pointing downwards and seems to be partly behind the upwards pointing triangle, is an example of amodal completion.

Quite a lot of research has gone into uncovering the mechanism that makes this optical illusion possible. In the brain two effects are in operation: Completion (either modal or amodal) and filling-in, which is known as the Troxler Effect.

The Troxler Effect is named after Swiss physician and philosopher Ignaz Paul Vital Troxler who made the discovery, in 1804, that rigidly fixating one's gaze on some element in the visual field can cause surrounding stationary images to seemingly slowly disappear or fade. The focus of attention, forces the brain to stop its constant back and forth drifting of the eye. Starved of the visual information this movement, known as saccades, provides the brain fills in the surrounding area from its own experienced understanding of how backgrounds work.

The Troxler Effect along with the Kanizsa Illusion show that our perception of reality can be guided by our attention and therefore shaped by any situation that either directs our attention for us or makes additional, excessive demands on our attention which reduce the amount of visual processing we can carry out.

Bibliography

Chapter 1

1. Taylor, Steve. (2020, January 8). The meaning of life – a psychologist's view. The Conversation. https://theconversation.com/the-meaning-of-life-a-psychologists-view-129274
2. Metz, Thaddeus, "The Meaning of Life", The Stanford Encyclopedia of Philosophy (Summer 2013 Edition), Edward N. Zalta (ed.), URL = https://plato.stanford.edu/archives/sum2013/entries/life-meaning/
3. Seachris, J., 2011, "Meaning of Life: The Analytic Perspective", in Internet Encyclopedia of Philosophy, J. Fieser and B. Dowden (eds.)
4. Morgan, Jessica & Farsides, Tom. (2009). Measuring Meaning in Life. Journal of Happiness Studies. 10. 197-214. 10.1007/s10902-007-9075-0.
5. Metz, Thaddeus. (2013). Meaning in Life: An Analytic Study.
6. Dezutter J, Casalin S, Wachholtz A, Luyckx K, Hekking J, Vandewiele W. Meaning in life: an important factor for the psychological well-being of chronically ill patients?. Rehabil Psychol. 2013;58(4):334-341. doi:10.1037/a0034393
7. Niu, Chen-Chun1; Huang, Hui-Man2*; Hung, Yun-Ying3; Lee, Hsiu-Li4 A Study of Interpersonal Intimacy and Meaning of Life Among Elderly Institutionalized Veterans, Journal of Nursing Research: December 2016 - Volume 24 - Issue 4 - p 311-320. doi: 10.1097/JNR.0000000000000130

Chapter 2

1. Women at Cambridge, Chapter 1 : The achievements that matter most, and why. https://www.cam.ac.uk/women-at-cambridge/chapters-and-themes/chapter-1-the-achievements-that-matter-most-and-why.
2. van Berkum, Jos. (2010). The brain is a prediction machine that cares about good and bad - Any implications for neuropragmatics?. Italian Journal of Linguistics, v.22, 181-208

(2010). 22.

3. Settles IH. When Multiple Identities Interfere: The Role of Identity Centrality. Personality and Social Psychology Bulletin. 2004;30(4):487-500. doi:10.1177/0146167203261885

4. Coverman, S. (1989). Role overload, role conflict, and stress: Addressing consequences of multiple role demands. Social Forces, 67(4), 965-982.

5. Ganzach, Y. (1997). Misleading interaction and curvilinear terms. Psychological Methods, 2(3), 235-247.

6. Grotevant, H. D. (1992). Assigned and chosen identity components. In G. R. Adams, T. P. Gullotta, & R. Montemayor (Eds.), Adolescent identity formation (Vol. 4, pp. 73-90). Newbury Park, CA: Sage.

7. Settles, I. H., Sellers, R. M., & Damas, A., Jr. (2002). One role or two? The function of psychological separation in role conflict. Journal of Applied Psychology, 87(3), 574-582.

Chapter 3

1. Doran, G. T. (1981). There's a S.M.A.R.T. way to write management's goals and objectives. Management Review. 70 (11): 35–36.

2. Zayas, Vivian & Mischel, Walter & Pandey, Gayathri. (2014). Mind and Brain in Delay of Gratification. 10.1037/14322-007. https://www.researchgate.net/publication/259332420_Mind_and_Brain_in_Delay_of_Gratification

3. Sokol-Hessner P, et al. (2009) Thinking like a trader selectively reduces individuals' loss aversion. Proc Natl Acad Sci USA 106(13):5035–5040.

4. Schwarz G (1978) Estimating the dimension of a model. Ann Stat 6(2):461–464.

5. Burnham KP, Anderson DR (1998) Model Selection and Inference (Springer, New York).

6. Wager TD, Davidson ML, Hughes BL, Lindquist MA, Ochsner KN (2008) Prefrontal-subcortical pathways mediating successful emotion regulation. Neuron 59(6):1037–1050.

7. Atlas LY, Bolger N, Lindquist MA, Wager TD (2010) Brain mediators of predictive cue effects on perceived pain. J Neurosci 30(39):12964–12977.

8. Jiang, M., Zou, Y., Xin, Q., et al., 2019. Dose-response relationship between body mass index and risks of all-cause mortality and disability among the elderly: a systematic review and meta-analysis. Clin. Nutr. 38, 1511–1523.

9. Kang, Y., Strecher, V.J., Kim, E.S., Falk, E.B., 2019. Purpose in life and conflict-related neural responses during health decision making. Health Psychol. 38, 545–552.

10. Kim, E.S., Sun, J.K., Park, N., Peterson, C., 2013. Purpose in life and reduced incidence of stroke in older adults: the health and retirement study. J. Psychosom. Res. 74, 427–432.

11. Kim, E.S., Strecher, V.J., Ryff, C.D., 2014. Purpose in life and use of preventive health care services. Proc. Natl. Acad. Sci. 111, 16331–16336.

12. TOMASELLO Michael 2008. Origins of Human Communication. Cambridge, MA: MIT Press.

13. TRUESWELL John C. & Michael K. TANENHAUS (eds.) 2005. Approaches to studying world-situated language use: Bridging the language-as-product and language-action traditions. Cambridge, MA: MIT Press.

14. VAN BERKUM Jos J. A. forthcoming. Prediction in language comprehension: Upcoming facts, signs, and moves [working title].

Chapter 4

1. Nevid JS. Psychology: Concepts and Applications. Belmont, CA: Wadsworth Cengage Learning; 2013.

2. Tranquillo J, Stecker M. Using intrinsic and extrinsic motivation in continuing professional education. Surg Neurol Int. 2016;7(Suppl 7):S197-9. doi:10.4103/2152-7806.179231

3. Hockenbury DH, Hockenbury SE. Discovering Psychology. Macmillan; 2010.

4. Zhou Y, Siu AF. Motivational intensity modulates the effects of positive emotions on set shifting after controlling physiological arousal. Scand J Psychol. 2015;56(6):613-21. doi:10.1111/sjop.12247

5. Myers DG. Exploring Social Psychology. New York, NY: McGraw Hill Education, 2015.

6. Siegling AB, Petrides KV. Drive: Theory and construct

validation. PLoS One. 2016;11(7):e0157295. doi:10.1371/
journal.pone.0157295

7. Lewina O. Lee, Peter James, Emily S. Zevon, Eric S. Kim,
Claudia Trudel-Fitzgerald, Avron Spiro, Francine Grodstein,
Laura D. Kubzansky. Optimism is associated with exceptional
longevity in 2 epidemiologic cohorts of men and women.
Proceedings of the National Academy of Sciences Sep 2019, 116
(37) 18357-18362; DOI: 10.1073/pnas.1900712116

8. Moschis, George P. (1976), "Social Comparison and Informal
Group Influence," Journal of Marketing Research, 13 (Au-gust),
237–44.

9. Muniz, Albert M. and Thomas C. O'Guinn (2001), "Brand
Community," Journal of Consumer Research, 27 (March), 412–
32. Nail, Paul R., Geoff MacDonald, and David A. Levy (2000),
"Proposal of a Four-Dimensional Model of Social Response,"
Psy-chological Bulletin, 126 (3), 454–70.

10. Katz, Daniel (1960), "The Functional Approach to the Study of
Attitudes," Public Opinion Quarterly, 24 (2), 163–204.

11. Kelley, Harold H. (1973), "The Process of Causal Attribution,"
American Psychologist, 28 (February), 107–28.

12. Kernis, Michael H. (1984), "Need for Uniqueness, Self-Schemas,
and Thought as Moderators of the False-Consensus Effect,"
Journal of Experimental Social Psychology, 20 (4), 350–62.

Chapter 5

1. Campbell AM. An increasing risk of family violence during the
Covid-19 pandemic: Strengthening community collaborations
to save lives. Forensic Science International. Reports.
2020;2:100089. doi:10.1016/j.fsir.2020.100089

2. Boatright, Mody C. "The Myth of Frontier Individualism." The
Southwestern Social Science Quarterly, vol. 22, no. 1, 1941, pp.
14–32. JSTOR, www.jstor.org/stable/42879677. Accessed 1 Mar.
2021.

3. Jaaniste, Tiina & Hayes, Brett & Goodenough, Belinda &
Baeyer, Carl. (2006). Effects of attentional direction, age, and
coping style on cold-pressor pain in children. Behaviour research
and therapy. 44. 835-48. 10.1016/j.brat.2005.03.013.

4. Parker SK, Bindl UK, Strauss K. Making Things Happen:

A Model of Proactive Motivation. Journal of Management. 2010;36(4):827-856. doi:10.1177/0149206310363732

5. Vallerand, Robert & Verner-Filion, Jeremie. (2013). Making People's Life Most Worth Living: On the Importance of Passion for Positive Psychology. Terapia Psicologica. 31. 35-48. 10.4067/S0718-48082013000100004.

6. Vallerand, R.J. The role of passion in sustainable psychological well-being. Psych Well-Being 2, 1 (2012). https://doi.org/10.1186/2211-1522-2-1

7. Osório, Carlos & Probert, Thomas & Jones, Edgar & Young, Allan & Robbins, Ian. (2016). Adapting to Stress: Understanding the Neurobiology of Resilience. Behavioral medicine (Washington, D.C.). 43. 10.1080/08964289.2016.1170661.

8. Russo SJ, Murrough JW, Han MH, Charney DS, Nestler EJ. Neurobiology of resilience. Nat Neurosci. 2012;15(11):1475-1484. doi:10.1038/nn.3234

9. Alibhai, Y. (1989), 'Community whitewash', The Guardian, 23 January.

10. Althusser, L. (1972), For Marx, Harmondsworth: Penguin.

11. Amin, S. (1989), Eurocentrism, London: Zed Books.

12. Anderson, B. (1983), Imagined Communities, London: Verso.

13. Ang, I. (1985), Watching Dallas, London: Methuen.

14. Ang, I. (1991), 'Global media/local meaning', Media Information Australia (62), November: 4–8.

15. Ang, I. (1992), 'Hegemony-in-trouble', in D.Petrie (ed.) Screening Europe, London: British Film Institute.

16. Ang, I. and Morley, D. (1989), 'Mayonnaise culture and other European follies', Cultural Studies, 3:133–44.

17. Asch, Solomon E. (1951), "Effects of Group Pressure upon the Modifications and Distortion of Judgments," in Groups, Leadership, and Men, ed. Harold Guetzkow, Pittsburgh: Carnegie.

18. Barker, Olivia (2004), "Everything Is So 5 Minutes Ago," USA Today, January 26, 1D.

Chapter 6

1. Rüdiger J. Seitz, Hans-Ferdinand Angel, Belief formation – A driving force for brain evolution, Brain and Cognition, Volume 140, 2020, 105548, ISSN 0278-2626, https://doi.org/10.1016/j.

bandc.2020.105548.

2. Sullivan BF, Schwebel AI. Relationship Beliefs and Expectations of Satisfaction in Marital Relationships: Implications for Family Practitioners. The Family Journal. 1995;3(4):298-305. doi:10.1177/1066480795034003

3. Anderson, S. A. , Russell, C. S. , & Schumm, W. R. (1983). Perceived marital quality and family life-cycle categories: A further analysis. Journal of Marriage and the Family, 45, 127-139.

4. Baucom, D. H. , & Epstein, N. (1990). Cognitive-behavioral marital therapy. New York: Brunner/Mazel.

5. Wiley, Clapp (2007). "The Jeff Cooper Legacy". American Rifleman. National Rifle Association. 155 (6): 44, 45, 58&60.

6. Olivos, Pablo & Aragones, Juan & Amerigo, Maria. (2011). The connectedness to nature scale and its relationship with environmental beliefs and identity. International Psychology Hispanic Journal. 4. 5-19. https://www.researchgate.net/publication/236172119_The_connectedness_to_nature_scale_and_its_relationship_with_environmental_beliefs_and_identity

7. Ponizovskiy V, Grigoryan L, Kühnen U, Boehnke K. Social Construction of the Value-Behavior Relation. Front Psychol. 2019;10:934. Published 2019 May 1. doi:10.3389/fpsyg.2019.00934

8. Morandini, James & Dar-Nimrod, Ilan. (2015). Essentialist Beliefs, Sexual Identity Uncertainty, Internalized Homonegativity and Psychological Wellbeing in Gay Men. Journal of Counseling Psychology.

9. Geoff Heath (2002) Does a theory of mind matter? The myth of totalitarian scientism, International Journal of Psychotherapy, 7:3, 185-220, DOI: 10.1080/1356908021000063187

10. Heath, A., Evans, G., & Martin, J. (1994). The Measurement of Core Beliefs and Values: The Development of Balanced Socialist/Laissez Faire and Libertarian/Authoritarian Scales. British Journal of Political Science, 24(1), 115-132. doi:10.1017/S0007123400006815

11. Morley, David & Robins, Kevin. (1997). Spaces of Identity : Global Media, Electronic Landscapes and Cultural Boundaries / D. Morley, K. Robins.. Geographical Review. 87. 10.2307/216048.

12. Berger, J. A., & Heath, C. (2007). Where Consumers Diverge

from Others: Identity Signaling and Product Domains. Journal of Consumer Research, 34 (2), 121-134. http://dx.doi. org/10.1086/519142

13. Gugerty, L., & Tirre, W. (1997). Situation awareness: A validation study and investigation of individual differences. Proceedings of the Human Factors and Ergonomics SocietyAnnual Meeting, 40, 564– 568. doi: 10.1177/154193129604001202

Chapter 7

1. Parks-Leduc, Laura & Feldman, Gilad & Bardi, Anat. (2014). Personality Traits and Personal Values: A Meta-Analysis. Personality and Social Psychology Review. 19. 10.1177/1088868314538548.

2. Schwartz, Shalom & Cieciuch, Jan & Vecchione, Michele & Davidov, Eldad & Fischer, Ronald & Beierlein, Constanze & Ramos, Alice & Verkasalo, Markku & Lönnqvist, Jan-Erik & Demirutku, Kursad & dirilen-gumus, Ozlem & Konty, Mark. (2012). Refining the theory of basic individual values. Journal of Personality and Social Psychology. 103. 663-88. 10.1037/ a0029393.

3. Cieciuch, Jan & Schwartz, Shalom & Davidov, Eldad. (2015). Values, Social Psychology of.

4. Ponizovskiy V, Grigoryan L, Kühnen U, Boehnke K. Social Construction of the Value-Behavior Relation. Front Psychol. 2019;10:934. Published 2019 May 1. doi:10.3389/ fpsyg.2019.00934

5. Shalom H. Schwartz, Universals in the Content and Structure of Values: Theoretical Advances and Empirical Tests in 20 Countries, Editor(s): Mark P. Zanna, Advances in Experimental Social Psychology, Academic Press, Volume 25, 1992, Pages 1-65, ISSN 0065-2601, ISBN 9780120152254, https:// doi.org/10.1016/S0065-2601(08)60281-6. (https://www. sciencedirect.com/science/article/pii/S0065260108602816)

6. Noftle, Erik & Schnitker, Sarah & Robins, Richard. (2011). Character and Personality. 10.1093/ acprof:oso/9780195373585.003.0014.

7. West, Nalini Maria, "The Relationship Among Personality Traits,

Character Strengths, and Life Satisfaction in College Students. "
PhD diss., University of Tennessee, 2006. https://trace.tennessee.
edu/utk_graddiss/4271

8. Hirsh, Jacob & Mar, Raymond & Peterson, Jordan. (2012).
    Psychological Entropy: A Framework for Understanding
    Uncertainty-Related Anxiety. Psychological Review. 119. 304-
    320. 10.1037/a0026767.

9. W. Schuett, S. R. X. Dall, A. J. Wilson, N. J. Royle.
    Environmental transmission of a personality trait: foster parent
    exploration behaviour predicts offspring exploration behaviour
    in zebra finches. Biology Letters, 2013; 9 (4): 20130120 DOI:
    10.1098/rsbl.2013.0120

10. Sanchez-Roige S, Gray JC, MacKillop J, Chen CH, Palmer
    AA. The genetics of human personality. Genes Brain Behav.
    2018;17(3):e12439. doi:10.1111/gbb.12439

11. Krueger RF, South S, Johnson W, Iacono W. The heritability of
    personality is not always 50%: gene-environment interactions
    and correlations between personality and parenting. J Pers.
    2008;76(6):1485-1522. doi:10.1111/j.1467-6494.2008.00529.x

12. Burke NJ, Joseph G, Pasick RJ, Barker JC. Theorizing social
    context: rethinking behavioral theory. Health Educ Behav.
    2009;36(5 Suppl):55S-70S. doi:10.1177/1090198109335338

13. Matsumoto, David. (2008). Culture, Context, and Behavior.
    Journal of personality. 75. 1285-319. 10.1111/j.1467-
    6494.2007.00476.x.

14. Turner, Roy. (2017). Context-Mediated Behavior. Modélisation
    et utilisation du contexte. 17. 10.21494/ISTE.OP.2017.0131.

15. Elyasaf, Achiya. (2020). Context-Oriented Behavioral
    Programming. Information and Software Technology. 133.
    106504. 10.1016/j.infsof.2020.106504.

16. Self MW, Peters JC, Possel JK, Reithler J, Goebel R, Ris P, et al.
    (2016) The Effects of Context and Attention on Spiking Activity
    in Human Early Visual Cortex. PLoS Biol 14(3): e1002420.
    https://doi.org/10.1371/journal.pbio.1002420

17. August Corrons Giménez, Lluís Garay Tamajón, Analysis of the
    third-order structuring of Shalom Schwartz's theory of basic
    human values, Heliyon, Volume 5, Issue 6, 2019, e01797, ISSN
    2405-8440, https://doi.org/10.1016/j.heliyon.2019.e01797

Chapter 8

1. Caza, Arran & Caza, Brianna & Baloochi, Mehri. (2020). Resilient Personality: Is Grit a Source of Resilience?.
2. Eisenberg, N., Duckworth, A. L., Spinrad, T. L., & Valiente, C. (2014). Conscientiousness: Origins in childhood? Developmental Psychology, 50(5), 1331–1349. https://doi.org/10.1037/a0030977
3. Joshua J. Jackson and Brent W. Roberts. The Oxford Handbook of the Five Factor Model, Edited by Thomas A. Widiger. Print Publication Date: May 2017Subject: Psychology, Social PsychologyOnline Publication Date: Sep 2015DOI: 10.1093/oxfordhb/9780199352487.013.18
4. Chad E. Forbes, Joshua C. Poore, Frank Krueger, Aron K. Barbey, Jeffrey Solomon & Jordan Grafman (2014) The role of executive function and the dorsolateral prefrontal cortex in the expression of neuroticism and conscientiousness, Social Neuroscience, 9:2, 139-151, DOI: 10.1080/17470919.2013.871333
5. Takahashi, Yusuke & Zheng, Anqing & Yamagata, Shinji & Ando, Juko. (2021). Genetic and environmental architecture of conscientiousness in adolescence. Scientific Reports. 11. 10.1038/s41598-021-82781-5.
6. Rueter, AR, Abram, SV, MacDonald, AW, Rustichini, A, DeYoung, CG. The goal priority network as a neural substrate of Conscientiousness. Hum Brain Mapp. 2018; 39: 3574– 3585. https://doi.org/10.1002/hbm.24195
7. Zak PJ. Why inspiring stories make us react: the neuroscience of narrative. Cerebrum. 2015;2015:2. Published 2015 Feb 2.
8. Armstrong, Paul. (2019). Neuroscience, Narrative, and Narratology. Poetics Today. 40. 395-428. 10.1215/03335372-7558052.
9. Alhadabi, Amal & Karpinski, Aryn. (2019). Grit, self-efficacy, achievement orientation goals, and academic performance in University students. International Journal of Adolescence and Youth. 25. 1-18. 10.1080/02673843.2019.1679202.
10. Dutke, S. Remembered duration: Working memory and the reproduction of intervals. Perception & Psychophysics 67, 1404–1413 (2005). https://doi.org/10.3758/BF03193645

Chapter 9

1. Clausewitz, Carl von. On War, abridged version translated by Michael Howard and Peter Paret, edited with an introduction by Beatrice Heuser Oxford World's Classics (Oxford University Press, 2007) ISBN 978-0-19-954002-0
2. George Dimitriu (2018): Clausewitz and the politics of war: A contemporary theory, Journal of Strategic Studies. Doi: 10.1080/01402390.2018.1529567
3. The Last Punisher, Kevin Lancz, Ethan E. Rocke, Lindsey Lacz. Threshold Editions; Reprint edition (February 21, 2017), ISBN: 978-1501127267.
4. Laird, J. D., & Bresler, C. (1992). The process of emotional experience: A self-perception theory. In M. S. Clark (Ed.), Review of personality and social psychology, No. 13. Emotion (p. 213–234). Sage Publications, Inc.
5. Fred A. Yamoah, Adolf Acquaye, Unravelling the attitude-behaviour gap paradox for sustainable food consumption: Insight from the UK apple market, Journal of Cleaner Production, Volume 217,
6. 2019, Pages 172-184, ISSN 0959-6526, https://doi.org/10.1016/j.jclepro.2019.01.094.
7. Guyer, Joshua & Fabrigar, Leandre. (2015). The attitude-behavior link: A review of the history.
8. Amy J.C.; Cuddy, Matthew K. and Neffinger, J. (2013). Connect, Then Lead: To exert influence, you must balance competence with warmth. Harvard Business Review.
9. Andrade, S. M.; Fischer, A.L. and Stefano, S. R. (2015). Organizational and interpersonal trust as a dimension of organizational climate. BASE - Journal of Administration and Accounting of Unisinos. 12 (2): 155-166, April / June. DOI: 10.4013 / base.2015.122.06.
10. Correia, C.M.C. (2001). Semiosis and cognitive development: Study on the Strategies of Construction of the Sonic
11. Processes in Logical Sequences. (2001). 200 f. Dissertation (Master in Linguistics). Rio de Janeiro: UERJ.
12. Covey, S. R. (2002). Principle-based leadership. Rio de Janeiro: Campus.
13. Damasio, A. (1994). Descartes' Error: Emotion, Reason and Human Brain. New York: Avon Books.

14. Demo, P. (1995). Scientific Methodology in Social Sciences. 3. ed. São Paulo: Atlas.
15. Dictionary Priberam (2018). Stress. https://dicionario.priberam.org/estresse.
16. Engelman, D. (2015). Brain-Behavior Relationships in Systems of Emotion. The center for collaborative psychology and psychiatry. USA.

Chapter 10

1. Kubzansky LD, Sparrow D, Vokonas P, Kawachi I. Is the glass half empty or half full? A prospective study of optimism and coronary heart disease in the normative aging study. Psychosom Med. 2001 Nov-Dec;63(6):910-6. doi: 10.1097/00006842-200111000-00009. PMID: 11719629.
2. Sher S, McKenzie CR. Information leakage from logically equivalent frames. Cognition. 2006 Oct;101(3):467-94. doi: 10.1016/j.cognition.2005.11.001. Epub 2005 Dec 20. PMID: 16364278.
3. Bernecker, Katharina & Job, Veronika. (2019). Mindset Theory. 10.1007/978-3-030-13788-5_12.
4. Hashimoto T, Takeuchi H, Taki Y, Sekiguchi A, Nouchi R, Kotozaki Y, Nakagawa S, Miyauchi CM, Iizuka K, Yokoyama R, Shinada T, Yamamoto Y, Hanawa S, Araki T, Hashizume H, Kunitoki K, Kawashima R. Neuroanatomical correlates of the sense of control: Gray and white matter volumes associated with an internal locus of control. Neuroimage. 2015 Oct 1;119:146-51. doi: 10.1016/j.neuroimage.2015.06.061. Epub 2015 Jun 26. PMID: 26123375.
5. The Science of Fate: Why Your Future is More Predictable Than You Think, Hannah Critchlow, Hodder & Stoughton. 2019. ISBN-13 : 978-1473659285
6. Navigation-related structural change in the hippocampi of taxi drivers. Eleanor A. Maguire, David G. Gadian, Ingrid S. Johnsrude, Catriona D. Good, John Ashburner, Richard S. J. Frackowiak, Christopher D. Frith. Proceedings of the National Academy of Sciences Apr 2000, 97 (8) 4398-4403; DOI: 10.1073/pnas.070039597
7. Rosenthal, David. (1984). Armstrong's Causal Theory of Mind.

10.1007/978-94-009-6280-4_3.

Chapter 11

1. Alan s. waterman, seth j. schwartz and regina conti.the implications of two conceptions of happiness (hedonic enjoyment and eudaimonia) for the understanding of intrinsic motivation Journal of Happiness Studies (2008) 9:4179. DOI 10.1007/s10902-006-9020-7

2. Xing, Cai & Isaacowitz, Derek. (2006). Aiming at Happiness: How Motivation Affects Attention to and Memory for Emotional Images. Motivation and Emotion. 30. 243-250. 10.1007/s11031-006-9032-y.

3. Ceci, Michael & Phd, V.. (2015). A Correlational Study of Creativity, Happiness, Motivation, and Stress from Creative Pursuits. Journal of Happiness Studies. 17. 10.1007/s10902-015-9615-y.

4. Ahuvia, Aaron & Thin, Neil & Haybron, Daniel & Biswas-Diener, Robert & Timsit, Jean & Ricard, Mathieu. (2015). Happiness: An interactionist perspective. International Journal of Wellbeing. 5. 1-18. 10.5502/ijw.v5i1.1.

5. Dfarhud D, Malmir M, Khanahmadi M. Happiness & Health: The Biological Factors- Systematic Review Article. Iran J Public Health. 2014;43(11):1468-1477.

6. Ferreira, Fbio & Costa, Renato & Pereira, Leandro & Jerónimo, Carlos & Dias, Álvaro. (2018). The Relationship between Chemical of Happiness, Chemical of Stress, Leadership, Motivation and Organizational Trust: a Case Study on Brazilian Workers. Journal of international business and economics. 6. 10.15640/jibe.v6n2a8.

7. Berger M, Gray JA, Roth BL. The expanded biology of serotonin. Annu Rev Med. 2009;60:355-366. doi:10.1146/annurev. mcd.60.042307.110802

8. Graf H, Malejko K, Metzger CD, Walter M, Grön G, Abler B. Serotonergic, Dopaminergic, and Noradrenergic Modulation of Erotic Stimulus Processing in the Male Human Brain. J Clin Med. 2019;8(3):363. Published 2019 Mar 14. doi:10.3390/ jcm8030363

9. Schweitzer RD, O'Brien J, Burri A. Postcoital Dysphoria: Prevalence and Psychological Correlates. Sex Med. 2015;3(4):235-243. Published 2015 Oct 5. doi:10.1002/sm2.74

10. Becchio, cristina, mauro adenzato, and bruno g. bara. 2006. How the brain understands intention: Different neural circuits identify the componential features of motor and prior intentions. Consciousness and Cognition 15: 64 –74.

11. Jeannerod, Marc. 2006. Motor cognition: What actions tell to the self. Oxford: Oxford University Press.

12. Searle, John R. 2005. The self as a problem in philosophy and neurobiology. In The lost self: Pathologies of the brain and identity, edited by Todd E. Feinburg and Julian Paul Keenan. Oxford: Oxford University Press

13. Samuli Pöyhönen (2014) Intentional concepts in cognitive neuroscience, Philosophical Explorations, 17:1, 93-109, DOI: 10.1080/13869795.2013.742556

14. Rohr CS, Okon-Singer H, Craddock RC, Villringer A, Margulies DS (2013) Affect and the Brain's Functional Organization: A Resting-State Connectivity Approach. PLoS ONE 8(7): e68015. https://doi.org/10.1371/journal. pone.0068015

15. Csikszentmihalyi, Mihaly & Hunter, Jeremy. (2003). Happiness in Everyday Life: The Uses of Experience Sampling. Journal of Happiness Studies. 4. 185-199. 10.1023/A:1024409732742.

16. D. Kahneman, A. B. Krueger, D. A. Schkade, N. Schwarz, A. A. Stone, Science 306, 1776 (2004).

17. A. B. Krueger, D. A. Schkade, J. Public Econ. 92, 1833 (2008).

18. D. Kahneman, in Well-being: The foundations of hedonic psychology., D. Kahneman, E. Diener, N. Schwarz, Eds. (Russell Sage Foundation, New York, 1999), pp. 3-25

19. Killingsworth MA, Gilbert DT. A wandering mind is an unhappy mind. Science. 2010 Nov 12;330(6006):932. doi: 10.1126/science.1192439. PMID: 21071660.

20. Mogilner, Cassie & Bhattacharjee, Amit. (2014). Happiness from Ordinary and Extraordinary Experiences. Journal of Consumer Research. 41. 1-17. 10.1086/674724.

21. Van Berkum, J. J. A. (2010). The brain is a prediction machine that cares about good and bad - Any implications for neuropragmatics? Italian Journal of Linguistics, 22, 181-208

22. Kashdan TB, Rottenberg J. Psychological flexibility as a fundamental aspect of health. Clin Psychol Rev. 2010;30(7):865-878. doi:10.1016/j.cpr.2010.03.001

23. Alshami AM. Pain: Is It All in the Brain or the Heart? Curr Pain Headache Rep. 2019 Nov 14;23(12):88. doi: 10.1007/s11916-019-0827-4. PMID: 31728781.

24. Alcaino C, Knutson KR, Treichel AJ, Yildiz G, Strege PR, Linden DR, Li JH, Leiter AB, Szurszewski JH, Farrugia G, Beyder A (2018) A population of gut epithelial enterochromaffin cells is mechanosensitive and requires Piezo2 to convert force into serotonin release. Proc Natl Acad Sci U S A 115:E7632–E7641. doi:10.1073/pnas.1804938115 pmid:30037999

25. Subhash Kulkarni, Julia Ganz, James Bayrer, Laren Becker, Milena Bogunovic and Meenakshi Rao. Advances in Enteric Neurobiology: The "Brain" in the Gut in Health and Disease, Journal of Neuroscience 31 October 2018, 38 (44) 9346-9354; DOI: https://doi.org/10.1523/JNEUROSCI.1663-18.2018

26. Gorwood P. Neurobiological mechanisms of anhedonia. Dialogues Clin Neurosci. 2008;10(3):291-299. doi:10.31887/DCNS.2008.10.3/pgorwood

27. Yemiscigil, A., Vlaev, I. The bidirectional relationship between sense of purpose in life and physical activity: a longitudinal study. J Behav Med (2021). https://doi.org/10.1007/s10865-021-00220-2

28. Kim, Eric & Shiba, Koichiro & Boehm, Julia & Kubzansky, Laura. (2020). Sense of purpose in life and five health behaviors in older adults. Preventive Medicine. 139. 106172. 10.1016/j.ypmed.2020.106172.

29. Zhang, Zhanjia & Chen, Weiyun. (2019). A Systematic Review of the Relationship Between Physical Activity and Happiness. Journal of Happiness Studies. 20. 10.1007/s10902-018-9976-0.

30. Kop WJ, Synowski SJ, Newell ME, Schmidt LA, Waldstein SR, Fox NA. Autonomic nervous system reactivity to positive and negative mood induction: the role of acute psychological responses and frontal electrocortical activity. Biol Psychol. 2011;86(3):230-238. doi:10.1016/j.biopsycho.2010.12.003

31. Marshel JH, Kim YS, Machado TA, et al. Cortical layer-specific critical dynamics triggering perception. Science. 2019;365(6453):eaaw5202. doi:10.1126/science.aaw5202

32. Kumar, A., Killingsworth, M.A., & Gilovich, T. (2020). Spending on doing promotes more moment-to-moment happiness than spending on having. Journal of Experimental Social Psychology, 88, 103971.

33. Irwin, J.R., & Goodman, J.K. (2009). Happiness for Sale: Do Experiential Purchases Make Consumers Happier Than Material Purchases? Econometrics: Econometric & Statistical Methods - General eJournal.

34. Rutledge, R., de Berker, A., Espenhahn, S. et al. The social contingency of momentary subjective well-being. Nat Commun 7, 11825 (2016). https://doi.org/10.1038/ncomms11825

35. Rutledge, Robb & Skandali, Nikolina & Dayan, Peter & Dolan, Raymond. (2015). Dopaminergic Modulation of Decision Making and Subjective Well-Being. The Journal of neuroscience : the official journal of the Society for Neuroscience. 35. 9811-22. 10.1523/JNEUROSCI.0702-15.2015.

36. Rutledge, Robb & Skandali, Nikolina & Dayan, Peter & Dolan, Raymond. (2014). A computational and neural model of momentary subjective well-being. Proceedings of the National Academy of Sciences of the United States of America. 111. 10.1073/pnas.1407535111

Appendix

1. Kanizsa, G., and W. Gerbino, 1982. 'Amodal Completion: Seeing or Thinking?' in Organization and Representation in Perception, J. Beck (Ed.) Lawrence Earlbaum: NJ. pp. 167–190

2. Krauskopf, J., 1963. 'Effect of retinal image stabilization on the appearance of heterochromatic targets', Journal of the Optical Society of America Vol 53, pp. 741–744.

3. Myin, E., and L. De Nul, 2009. 'Filling-in', in T. Bayne, A. Cleeremans and P. Wilken (Eds), The Oxford Companion to Consciousness, OUP: Oxford.

4. Nanay, B., 2010. 'Perception and Imagination. Amodal Perception as Mental Imagery', Philosophical Studies Vol 150 pp. 239-254.

5. Pessoa, L., E. Thompson and A. Noë, 1998. 'Finding out about filling-in: A guide to perceptual completion for visual science

and the philosophy of perception', Behavioral and Brain Sciences
21 pp. 723-802.

Index

Page left blank on purpose

Page left blank on purpose

Page left blank on purpose

Page left blank on purpose